A Guide to

The Norton Reader

EIGHTH EDITION

The Editors of *The Norton Reader*, Eighth Edition

Arthur M. Eastman, General Editor
Virginia Polytechnic Institute and State University

Caesar R. Blake
University of Toronto

Hubert M. English, Jr.
University of Michigan

Joan E. Hartman
College of Staten Island, City University of New York

Alan B. Howes
University of Michigan

Robert T. Lenaghan
University of Michigan

Leo F. McNamara
University of Michigan

Linda H. Peterson
Yale University

James Rosier
University of Pennsylvania

A Guide to

The Norton Reader

EIGHTH EDITION

Joan E. Hartman
College of Staten Island, City University of New York

Linda H. Peterson
Yale University

W. W. NORTON & COMPANY
New York   London

ISBN 0-393-96196-6

W. W. Norton & Company, Inc., 500 Fifth Avenue, New York, N. Y.
10110

1 2 3 4 5 6 7 8 9 10

Contents

LANGUAGE AND COMMUNICATION

AN ALBUM OF STYLES

SIGNS OF THE TIMES

Index of Rhetorical Modes and Strategies

Rhetorical Modes

NARRATION

Maya Angelou: *Graduation* (NR 19, SE 11, G 4)
Jeremy Bernstein: *SN-1987 A* (NR 981)
Malcolm Cowley: *The View from 80* (NR 242)
Robertson Davies: *Ham and Tongue* (NR 1125, SE 689, G 174)
Annie Dillard: *Terwilliger Bunts One* (NR 147, SE 56, G 17)
Kildare Dobbs: *Gallipoli* (NR 795)
Loren Eiseley: *The Brown Wasps* (NR 49, SE 40, G 11)
M. F. K. Fisher: *Moment of Wisdom* (NR 205, SE 132, G 37)
Langston Hughes: *Salvation* (NR 1196, SE 727, G 183)
Samuel Johnson: *Letter to Lord Chesterfield* (NR 657)
Barry Lopez: *The Stone Horse* (NR 774)
Fredelle Maynard: *And Therefore I Have Sailed the Seas...*
    (NR 38, SE 29, G 10)
Joyce Maynard: *Four Generations* (NR 38, SE 26, G 8)
David McCullough: *The Unexpected Mrs. Stowe* (NR 103)
Margaret Mead: *Home and Travel* (NR 153, SE 75, G 24)
N. Scott Momaday: *The Way to Rainy Mountain*
    (NR 158, SE 80, G 25)
Richard Sewell: *A Sense of the Ending* (NR 1238)
Gary Soto: *The Pie* (NR 647, SE 409, G 109)
Wallace Stegner: *The Town Dump* (NR 10)
Dylan Thomas: *Memories of Christmas* (NR 1, SE 1, G 1)
James Thurber: *University Days* (NR 290, SE 163, G 46)
Barbara Tuchman: *"This Is the End of the World": The Black
    Death* (NR 754, G 125)
Eudora Welty: *One Writer's Beginnings*
    (NR 1043, SE 648, G 165)
Richard S. Westfall: *The Career of Isaac Newton:
    A Scientific Life in the Seventeenth Century*
    (NR 995)
E. B. White: *Once More to the Lake* (NR 55, SE 47, G 13)

DESCRIPTION

EXPOSITION

Essays That Compare and Contrast

Essays That Classify and Divide

Essays That Analyze Cause/Effect

Jerome S. Bruner: *Freud and the Image of Man* (NR 173)
Edward Hallett Carr: *The Historian and His Facts*
      (NR 833, SE 497, G 134)
Lord Chesterfield: *Letter to His Son* (NR 658)
Carl Cohen: *The Case for the Use of Animals in Biochemical
      Research* (NR 691)
William Faulkner: *Nobel Prize Award Speech*
      (NR 438, SE 281, G 76)
Paul Fussell: *Thank God for the Atom Bomb*
      (NR 711, SE 433, G 120)
Willard Gaylin: *What You See Is the Real You*
      (NR 675, SE 414, G 112)
Stephen Jay Gould: *Darwin's Middle Road*
      (NR 1013, SE 617, G 157)
Stephen Jay Gould: *Our Allotted Lifetimes*
      (NR 260, SE 148, G 41)
Stephen Jay Gould: *The Terrifying Normalcy of AIDS*
      (NR 702, SE 424, G 117)
S. I. Hayakawa: *Sex Is Not a Spectator Sport* (NR 1123)
Thomas Jefferson: *Original Draft of the
      Declaration of Independence* (NR 124,
      SE 563, G 145)
Thomas Jefferson and Others: *The Declaration
      of Independence* (NR 928, SE 567, G 145)
Martin Luther King, Jr.: *Letter from Birmingham Jail*
      (NR 886, SE 538, G 142)
Joseph Wood Krutch: *The Most Dangerous Predator* (NR 630)
Aldo Leopold: *Thinking Like a Mountain* (NR 628, SE 372, G 99)
Michael Levin: *The Case for Torture* (NR 677, SE 421, G 115)
Abraham Lincoln: *The Gettysburg Address*
      (NR 433, SE 277, G 73)
Abraham Lincoln: *Second Inaugural Address*
      (NR 922, SE 571, G 147)
Barry Lopez: *The Stone Horse* (NR 774)
Nancy Mairs: *Who Are You?* (NR 392, SE 247, G 60)
Richard Mitchell: *The Voice of Sisera* (NR 373, SE 221, G 52)
Joyce Carol Oates: *On Boxing* (NR 1138)
Plato: *The Allegory of the Cave* (NR 1153, SE 734, G 185)
Tom Regan: *The Case for Animal Rights* (NR 680)
Adrienne Rich: *Taking Women Students Seriously*
      (NR 295, SE 169, G 47)

Rhetorical Strategies

TITLE, AND OPENING AND CLOSING PARAGRAPHS

THESIS, DEVELOPMENT, AND SUPPORT

ORGANIZATION

PERSONA

Preface: To the Instructor

We have prepared this *Guide* in an attempt to offer collegial advice about use of *The Norton Reader*. Sometimes, we have drawn on materials from earlier *Guides*, retaining entries we found imaginative and practicable but making changes we thought likely to produce better classroom discussion. More often, we have written completely new entries, drawing on our combined experiences as writing teachers and our enthusiasm for essays new to the eighth edition. Not every suggestion will work for every instructor, nor will every writing assignment work for every student. But we have tried hard to be helpful—even when that has meant telling each other, "That won't work."

In conceiving the *Guide*, we have kept in mind the various kinds of writing courses for which *The Norton Reader* is well suited. One model for freshman composition calls essentially for serious, solid essays that first-year college students will enjoy reading and writing about. Textbooks for such courses are often labeled "liberal arts readers," suggesting that they introduce students to the liberal arts curriculum even as they improve critical thinking and writing. Whether or not you use the label, we think *The Norton Reader* ideal for such a course, and we have tried to suggest discussion questions and writing assignments that will engage students seriously in significant issues, in and out of the academy.

The Norton Reader works well in other kinds of writing courses, too, including those that focus on writing in the disciplines and those that focus on the essay form itself. Writing across the curriculum, one of the major pedagogical movements of the last decade, has reshaped the thinking of many of us who teach composition; it has reminded us not only of the importance of writing to learn but also of the discipline-specific nature of academic discourse. For instructors who use a writing-across-the-curriculum approach, the second half of *The Norton Reader* will prove especially valuable—and we hope our suggestions in the *Guide* will too. We have tried to send students back to sources, for example, to see how a professional historian works or to compare the prose of an environmentalist writing for a lay audience with his prose for fellow academics. We have tried also to construct brief writing assignments that ask students to locate their own sources and document them. And, for units representing a range of discourse, we have tried to include questions that get at discourse conventions within disciplines, as well as at rhetorical options that individual writers may—or may not—choose to exercise.

Finally, *The Norton Reader* offers a superb resource for courses that focus on the essay as a literary and social genre. The early sections of the *Reader*—"Personal Report," "People, Places," and "Signs of the Times"—reproduce some of the best essays and essayists of the last half century, whereas the later sections include many fine examples of what is often called "the literature of fact." In writing the *Guide,* we have retained questions with a literary or generic slant—questions about style, tone, persona, and rhetorical techniques—and we have suggested assignments that give students the opportunity to experiment with various forms of the essay genre. But we have also added questions that explore the personal, social, and political uses of the essay—so that classes can, if their instructors feel so inclined, think about how an essay situates itself at a historical moment for a specific rhetorical purpose. The *Guide* follows the contents of *The Norton Reader,* Eighth Edition Shorter, and provides critical material for every selection in that edition. It can, of course, be used with the Regular Edition, and our entries sometimes suggest comparisons with essays only in that longer edition. The "Index of Rhetorical Modes and Strategies" (pp. i–viii) cites page references for both versions (NR = Regular Edition, SE = Shorter Edition, G = Guide). The rhetorical index lists all 124 essays in the Shorter Edition and is intended to help instructors who prefer to organize their courses by rhetorical modes. Following this introduction is the essay that opens the *Reader,* "To Students: Reading and Writing with *The Norton Reader*" (p. 00), reprinted here for convenience. Its brief comments, intended to offer practical advice on reading essays, generating ideas, and composing and revising essays, might be assigned to students as introductory reading.

We hope each *Guide* entry will serve as a springboard for questions and observations, the instructors' and the students'. Entries consist of three parts:

1. An introduction to the essay and the author, which may be supplemented with the biographical sketches in the "Appendix" to the *Reader*.
2. "Analytical Considerations," which take up matters of form and content and rhetoric and style and which are meant to help instructors plan their syllabus and class discussions.
3. "Suggested Writing Assignments," which supplement assignments in the *Reader* itself and draw on key excerpts from the work, other essays related in theme or style, topics that touch students' lives, and issues central to liberal education—all with the aim of giving students provocative, wide-ranging possibilities for writing.

We hope you will find most if not all our suggestions in the *Guide* useful. They represent the collective wisdom of former authors of the *Guide*, most notably Bradford Snow, Wayne E. Blankenship, and Robert E. Hosmer, Jr.; the co-editors of *The Norton Reader* itself; our wise and most patient editor at Norton, Julia A. Reidhead; and our colleagues at our home institutions and in the profession at large.

Joan E. Hartman, *College of Staten Island,*
City University of New York

Linda H. Peterson, *Yale University*

To Students: Reading and Writing with *The Norton Reader*

This is the eighth edition of *The Norton Reader;* its first edition goes back to 1965. The editors have put together a selection of essays on a range of subjects, some familiar, others more specialized. You'll find the first kind in sections like "Personal Report," "People, Places," and "Signs of the Times," the second in sections like "Science," "Literature and the Arts," and "Philosophy and Religion." Some of these sections go back to the first edition: "Personal Report" opened the first as it still does the eighth. Others have come and gone: in this edition, for example, we've dropped a section called "Mind"— transferring some of its essays to "Human Nature"—and added a section called "Nature and the Environment." Some essays have appeared in all eight editions of *The Norton Reader:* E. B. White's "Once More to the Lake," for example, and Jonathan Swift's "A Modest Proposal." Others—about one-third—are new to this edition. You'll find some of the essays longer, some shorter; some formal, some informal; some calculatedly challenging, some simpler.

The editors—now nine of us—search widely in order to include a range of authors. Although most of the essays are contemporary, some are older; although most of them are written in English, a few are translated from other languages. You'll hear in them male and female voices; American, British, and Canadian voices; African-American, Asian-American, American Indian, and Spanish-American voices. What the essays have in common is excellence: at least three editors, without actually defining good writing to ourselves or for each other, have agreed on the inclusion of each essay. We find their subjects important, timely, timeless, engaging. We find their authors, sometimes well known, sometimes less well known, speaking with authority and, often, seeing with a distinctive angle of vision. We find their writing convincing and clear, their style lean when elaboration is not required but adequate to complexity. The essays are not invariably simple to read: they originally appeared in publications read by informed and educated general readers.

The editors have provided a large number of essays, more than any instructor will assign during a semester. This time the regular edition contains 207; the shorter, 121. The organization, by kinds of writing and kinds of subjects, is loose. We know that there are many kinds of college writing courses; we know that instructors link reading and writing in a variety of ways. Our aim in *The Norton Reader* is to accommodate all or most of them. In consequence, we limit our editorial presence. You'll find, after some but not all of the essays, questions addressed to you as readers and others addressed to you as writers. We intend them to focus your reading of the essays: questions addressed to readers ask about the essays' content, meaning, and argument; questions addressed to writers ask about their authors' strategies—how they present their content and how they make their meanings clear. In the questions addressed to you as writers there's also at least one follow-up writing assignment—out of the many assignments that are possible. We leave it to your instructors to direct you through the essays, to decide which ones to assign and how to use them.

Reading

We hope that, in addition to following your instructors' assignments, you'll also follow your own interests. But we don't count on it. Putting essays in a textbook, even one called a "Reader," makes reading them artificial. They were written for and read by readers who read them naturally: because they wanted to know—or know more—about their subjects, because they knew—or knew of—their authors, or because the essays, appearing in publications they ordinarily read, tempted them to launch into unfamiliar subjects written by authors they had never heard of. Outside the classroom, readers bring their own interests and motives to reading; inside the classroom, you are left to generate your own in response to assignments.

As editors, we've tried to make available some of the choices available to the original readers of these essays. Information about them appears in two places. A footnote at the beginning of each essay tells you when and where it first appeared and, if it began as a talk, when and where it was delivered and to whom. Maya Angelou's "Graduation," for example, is a chapter from her autobiography, *I Know Why the Caged Bird Sings,* published in 1969; Scott Russell Sanders' "Looking at Women" was published in a journal called the

Georgia Review in 1989; Francis Bacon's "Of Revenge" was published in a collection of his essays called, simply, *Essays*, in 1625; Chief Seattle's "Address" (which is translated) was delivered in response to a treaty offered to his people in 1854; Frances FitzGerald's "Rewriting American History" comes from her *America Revised*, published in *The New Yorker* and then as a book in 1979. We don't, however, explain the differences between the *Georgia Review* and *The New Yorker;* the first, a noncommercial journal published three times a year by the University of Georgia, has fewer and presumably more select and self-selected readers than *The New Yorker*, a commercial magazine published weekly. If more information about context helps situate you in relation to what you are reading, ask your instructors. As editors, we could swamp a smaller number of essays with additional information about their contexts, but we prefer to include more essays and keep contextual information spare.

A section called "Authors" at the end of *The Norton Reader* provides biographical and bibliographical information about the authors whose essays we include. Outside the classroom, we may know something about the authors we read before we read them, or we may encounter them as unknowns. We may choose to let them speak for themselves, to see what we can discover about them as they do. Sometimes knowing who they are and where their voices come from helps us to hear them and to grasp what they say—but sometimes it doesn't. Putting biographical information at the end gives you, in a textbook, something like the choices ordinary readers have as to how much knowledge about authors to bring to their reading.

An index listing essays by title and by author also appears at the end of *The Norton Reader*. It's of course useful for locating essays; it's also useful for identifying multiple essays by the same author. The regular edition includes multiple selections by eighteen authors; the shorter, multiple selections by more authors, among them, for example, Joan Didion, Gretel Ehrlich, Stephen Jay Gould, and George Orwell. When you enjoy your encounter with particular authors, it's worth looking in the index to see if we've included additional essays by them; following an author provides motives for reading such as ordinary readers have.

In addition to information about contexts and authors, we also provide, in footnotes, explanations of material in the essays themselves. Our rules for annotation go something like this: (1) *Don't* define words, except foreign words, that appear in desk dictionaries. You can go to yours or, more sensibly, guess from context. If an unfamiliar word is central to the meaning of an essay, the author is likely to define it. (2) *Do* provide information about people, places, works, theories, and unfamiliar things. For example, for Maya Angelou's "Graduation," we explain Gabriel Prosser, Nat Turner, and Harriet Tubman (but not Abraham Lincoln and Christopher Columbus); Stamps (it's not immediately clear that it's an Arkansas town); and the poem "Invictus." For Frances FitzGerald's "Rewriting American History," we explain socialist realism and American nuclear bomb tests in the Pacific. We don't always agree among ourselves on what needs annotation or how much information constitutes an explanation. (In this we're not unique: all annotators make assumptions about the information readers they don't fully know bring to their reading.) Our experience in the classroom helps us estimate the annotation you need. But you can be sure that we'll fail you in some places and affront you in others by explaining what you find obvious. When we fail you, ask your instructors for help; when we affront you, take our efforts as well intentioned. Again, rather than swamping a smaller number of essays with annotation, we keep it spare.

Our last rule for notes is the trickiest. (3) Explain, don't interpret—that is, provide information but leave readers to decide how authors frame and engage the material we explain and how it contributes to their meanings. Francis Bacon's "Of Revenge," for example, ends: "Public revenges are for the most part fortunate; as that for the death of Caesar; for the death of Pertinax; for the death of Henry the third of France; and many more. But in private revenges it is not so, Nay rather, vindictive persons live the life of witches; who as they are mischievous, so end they infortunate." We explain Pertinax and Henry III (but not Caesar). You sensibly could guess, without annotation, that all three were, first, public persons, and second, assassinated. We give dates—Pertinax assassinated in 193, Henry III in 1589—but leave you to consider what Bacon's illustrations, ranging over time, contribute to his meaning. We also leave you to work out what made these revenges "for the most part fortunate," because Bacon himself, with his terse, elliptical style, demands that you do. He contrasts these public revenges with private revenges that are "not so," that is, not for the most part fortunate, and then points out the consequences for the assassins themselves, who end unfortunately. To work out the meanings engaged by Bacon's illustrations is to interpret rather than to explain. Working out meanings is the work of readers and, in the classroom, of communities of readers and instructors.

Finally, of course, we include the authors' own notes, distinguishing theirs from ours by adding their names in square brackets. In general, authors' notes are infrequent: extensive notes indicate academic writers addressing other academics within their disciplines rather than nonacademic writers addressing general readers. This edition of *The Norton Reader* includes a report published in a scientific journal, "Handgun Regulations, Crime, Assaults, and Homicide: A Tale of Two Cities," from the *New England Journal of Medicine*, which has extensive notes. Scientific reports accessible to general readers are not easy to find. This one stands in useful contrast to the essays by Stephen Jay Gould that we also include: he's a scientist who writes for general readers, who popularizes science. Among the differences between the handgun report and Gould's essays is the presence (or the absence) of authors' notes.

Assignments in *The Norton Reader* will motivate you to "read" but won't make you readers, that is, persons who bring to what they read their own interests and who are ready to engage in the activity of making meaning out of words encountered on a page. Reading is a solitary enterprise and making meaning somewhat mysterious. Watch yourself as you do it. Try to notice what happens when you succeed and when you fail, for failure is as instructive as success. Ordinarily you are the sole judge of both. Short-answer tests elicit only your superficial comprehension. Writing about what you read, in essay examinations or papers, tests your comprehension of large structures. But sentence to sentence, paragraph to paragraph, your comprehension is manifest only to you. Mark up your texts as a record: where do you deal confidently with meaning, where tentatively and where do you drift away, either willfully or inadvertently? And what can you learn about yourself as a reader through this kind of marking?

Because assigned reading is shared reading, class discussion can move the making of meaning from a solitary to a social enterprise. The classroom provides a community of readers and opportunities to demystify reading. What interests and motives do we, students and instructors alike, bring to texts? What strategies do we employ when we read? Are there other, more useful ones? What meanings are common to us, what meanings individual? What is responsive and responsible reading? When do individual meanings become irresponsible, and how do we decide? These are questions that concern writers as well as readers: making meaning by writing is the flip side of making it by reading. In neither enterprise is meaning passed from hand to hand like nickels, dimes, and quarters.

Writing

Making meaning by writing is less mysterious than making it by reading. Most instructors of writing, however they choose to link reading and writing, emphasize what's called process. Process refers to working in stages on multiple drafts; product refers to final drafts. Multiple drafts provide evidence for what we do and how we do it. Student writers seldom have time to proceed through as many drafts as do professional writers and experienced writers. But learning to distribute the time you have over several drafts rather than one will turn out to be the most efficient use of it.

Experienced writers know they can't do everything at once: assemble material; assess its usefulness; disperse it in sections, paragraphs, and sentences; and write it out in well-formed sentences. Student writers, however, often expect to produce a finished single draft. If that's what you expect of yourself, then a writing course is a good place to change your expectations and cultivate more sensible and profitable practices. When you try to produce a finished single draft, you are likely to thin out your evidence and disperse it in simple ways; lock yourself into structures you can't change even if in the course of writing you discover new meanings and write lumpy sentences that need to be reformed. In addition, single-draft writing, when you're aiming for something reasonably thoughtful and deserving of a respectable grade, is harder than multiple-draft writing and no quicker.

The process experienced writers go through when they write is something like this. They start with freewriting, brainstorming, listing, or whatever other heuristic devices—that is, means of discovering what to write—that they have learned work for them. They try out what they have to say in rough drafts. As they shape their material, they find what it means and what they want it to mean, as they find what it means and what they want it to mean, they figure out how to shape it—shape and meaning are reciprocal. Large and small are also reciprocal: they work back and forth among complete drafts and smaller units—sections and paragraphs in longer drafts, paragraphs in shorter. As shape and meaning come together, they refine still smaller units, that is, sentences, phrases, even words.

Then, when they have a draft that in some sense satisfies them, they turn themselves around. Having written for themselves and made their own meaning, they attend to writing for others, to transmitting what they mean. They try to distance themselves from themselves and from their draft by putting it aside for a time, if they can, and by imagining themselves as readers other than themselves bringing to what they've written other interests, other motives. Writing for oneself takes commitment: we have to turn off the censor that inhibits our writing and embarrasses us with what we have written. Writing for others takes skepticism: we have to turn the censor back on—or find a reader or readers who will dramatize for us the experience of making meaning from our draft and help us to see how we have been understood and misunderstood.

This is the rough sequence of tasks experienced writers perform in overlapping stages. They revise at all stages and their revisions are substantial. What inexperienced writers call revision—tinkering with surface features by rewording, pruning, and correcting—experienced writers call editing and proofreading. These tasks they do at the end, when they are ready to stop revising and prepare what they call a final draft; if larger elements of a draft need repair, it's too soon to work on smaller elements.

To distance yourself from your own drafts or to respond to someone else's, individually and in groups, think about a hierarchy of questions.

1. When you write in response to an assignment, ask,"Did I do what I was told to do?" When you write on a subject you choose yourself, ask, "Did I do what I promised to do in the introduction?" In the second instance, you can revise your introduction to make a promise you keep: experienced writers expect to revise their introductions radically as their drafts take shape. In the first instance, you'll have to decide whether or not what you have written is a reasonable substitute for the assignment and, if it is, how to introduce it honestly.

2. Then ask, "Is the material I have included appropriate? Have I included enough, and have I interpreted it fairly and adequately?" Appropriateness is more or less straightforward. Inclusiveness is problematic. Ordinarily, experienced writers are more inclusive than student writers. You may find the essays in *The Norton Reader* dense and overspecific; your instructors, on the other hand, may find your essays skimpy and underspecific. Experienced writers thicken their writing with particulars to transmit their meanings and engage readers' recognition, understanding, and imagination. Because they are more in control of their writing than student writers, they are able to be more inclusive, to sustain multiple examples and illustrations.

Responsible writers want to interpret material fairly; slanted interpretation is the stock-in-trade of advertisers and hucksters.

Interpreting material fairly means maintaining its emphases and distorting its inflections as little as possible. In general, experienced writers interpret adequately and student writers underinterpret. One way of assessing adequacy is looking at quotations. How many are there? (Experienced writers ordinarily use fewer than student writers.) How necessary are they? (Experienced writers paraphrase more than they quote.) How well are they integrated? (Experienced writers introduce quotations by explaining who is speaking, where the voice is coming from, and what to listen for; they finish off quotations by linking them to what follows.)

3. Then ask, "Is the material well deployed?" Writing involves putting readers in possession of interrelated material in a temporal order: readers read from start to finish. Sometimes material explained near the end might better be explained near the beginning; sometimes material explained near the beginning might better be postponed. When paragraphs follow each other, transitional words like *therefore* may not be necessary; when they don't, missing connections can't be supplied by *therefore*.

4. Then ask, "At the sentence level, which sentences unfold unproblematically and which sentences make readers stumble?" Readers who can identify what makes them stumble as they read your writing will teach you more about well-formed sentences than any set of rules for forming them.

Writing, unlike reading, is both a solitary and a social enterprise: while we compose and revise by ourselves, we eventually put our drafts into circulation. A writing classroom, at best, introduces social dimensions into the process, as students put less-than-final drafts into circulation and receive responses to them. It provides a community of readers to read each other's writing as well as the writing of professional and experienced writers in a text such as *The Norton Reader*. Honing one's skills as a reader on professional writing is good training: it will help you to respond to the writing of less-experienced writers, others' writing and your own.

A Guide to

The Norton Reader

EIGHTH EDITION

PERSONAL REPORT

DYLAN THOMAS

Memories of Christmas

The Norton Reader, p. 1; Shorter Edition, p. 1

Dylan Thomas' "Memories of Christmas" is a nostalgic recollection of childhood Christmases in Wales. Thomas recollects a lot: sights, sounds, events, persons, toys, food, the weather. And he writes about it "poetically," with inventive and evocative language and carefully worked rhythmic sentences. The central portion of "Memories of Christmas" (paragraphs 14–39) is a composite account. Ordinarily students thin out detail and specificity when asked to write composite accounts; they write better when asked to write particular accounts—of last Christmas or the "Christmas when I was ten." Reading "Memories of Christmas," you will want to call their attention to Thomas' density, indeed, to his heaping up of details. You will also want them to notice that his central composite account is framed by two particular accounts, one of the Prothero fire, the other of Christmas caroling. The first two (the Prothero fire and the composite account) are introduced by the metaphoric snowball Thomas describes in paragraph 2: It's a "wool-white bell-tongued ball of holidays" in paragraph 3, and "that bright white snowball of Christmas gone" in paragraph 14. The third (the caroling) is introduced more simply: "And I remember that we went singing carols once" (paragraph 40).

Analytical Considerations

1. Although Thomas talks about Christmas from a child's perspective, he uses the resources of his adult, and unusually expressive, language to recreate it; he is primarily known as a poet. You might ask students to mark vivid sentences and passages. You might also use this exercise to identify techniques like metaphor, simile, compounding, etc.
2. The first two paragraphs contain one sentence each. You might look at their syntax with students and figure out how they are put

together. You might also set up one or the other as a syntactical skeleton and have students, probably in groups, flesh it out with their own details. What are the uses of such sentences?

3. Although "Memories of Christmas" is an account of personal experience, it reveals very little about the person. What does it reveal and what does it not reveal?

Suggested Writing Assignments

1. Use Thomas' essay as a model for writing your own recollection of childhood. Take a recurring event, perhaps a holiday, perhaps a more ordinary day like the first or last day of school. You might make Thomas' point, that these days were so much alike you can no longer distinguish among them.

2. Single out a particular recurring event (above) with some attention to what made it stand out in memory among other days like it.

3. Write an essay about the power of memory. Use episodes from your own life to illustrate the points you make.

4. Write an essay about the power of memory for Thomas in "Memories of Christmas" and Margaret Laurence in "Where the World Began" (NR 6, SE 6). You may want to make this essay a formal comparison.

MARGARET LAURENCE

Where the World Began

The Norton Reader, p. 6; Shorter Edition, p. 6

The late Margaret Laurence was a Canadian novelist, short-story writer, and essayist; this essay, first published in *Maclean's* magazine, was reprinted in *Heart of a Stranger* (1976), a collection of autobiographical essays. "Where the World Began" bears comparison with Dylan Thomas' "Memories of Christmas" (NR 1, SE 1): both are composite accounts. Laurence's account is broader than Thomas' in that she recollects an entire childhood, so to speak. Nevertheless, she also limits herself to the town and the surrounding country, and the people who appear briefly are townsfolk, not family. "Where the World Began" is developed by association. Some paragraphs are organized by time: "In winter" (paragraph 4) and "Summers" (paragraph 5). Others are organized by topic: "the outside world" (paragraph 6), the town (paragraph 7), and "oddities" (paragraph 8).

Laurence's attitude toward the past she recreates is more complex than Thomas toward his. The past impinges on the present, and her past, which she wanted to put behind her, stayed with her. Her formulations of how and why it stayed are arresting: "I did not know then that I would carry the land and town all my life within my skull" (paragraph 12) or "it was here that I learned the sight of my particular eyes" (paragraph 20). Her re-creation of the past leads her to reflect on herself as a Canadian and to recognize that, however ambivalent her connection with Canada and Canadians, she is bound to the land itself.

Analytical Considerations

1. Like Thomas in "Memories of Christmas," Laurence heaps up detail. It is predominantly visual (as description often is). You might ask students to notice particular examples and connect them with Laurence's claims about seeing and learning to see.
2. Although "Where the World Began" is an account of personal experience, it focuses on the experience of place, not the experience of people. What does it reveal about Laurence and how? What does it not reveal?

Suggested Writing Assignments

1. Use Laurence's essay as a model for writing your own recollection of a place that was and is important to you.
2. Write an essay about the power of memory. Use episodes from your own life to illustrate the points you make.
3. Write an essay about the power of memory for Margaret Laurence in "Where the World Began" and Dylan Thomas in "Memories of Christmas." You may want to make this essay a formal comparison.
4. "I have lived in Africa and England, but splendid as both can be, they do not have the power to move me in the same way as, for example, that part of southern Ontario where I spent four months last summer in a cedar cabin beside a river" (paragraph 16). Read an essay about another place in Laurence's *Heart of a Stranger* (1976) and compare her treatment of it with her treatment of place in "Where the World Began."

MAYA ANGELOU

Graduation

The Norton Reader, p. 19; Shorter Edition, p. 11

Maya Angelou's "Graduation," taken from the first volume of her autobiography, *I Know Why the Caged Bird Sings,* is a particular account, its focus a unique event: her graduation from eighth grade in Stamps, Arkansas, in 1940. The essay is organized by time, chronological time. The sequence of events Angelou describes begins with the town's, her family's, and her own preparations for graduation and culminates in the ceremony itself. Chronology is a natural ordering and, in Angelou's hands, an effective one. You might ask students to look at "real" time and "fictional" time in "Graduation"; the "real" time of events leading up to the ceremony is compressed in relation to the "real" time of the ceremony itself, or, conversely, the "fictional" time of the ceremony is extended with description, dialogue, and the young Angelou's own responses. Chronology is a form that students handle well, provided they see that "real" time is malleable and in their control. It also offers them opportunities for significant revision. Yet the chronologically ordered events of "Graduation" are themselves an implicit flashback in that the narrative voice belongs to the mature Angelou looking back in 1969 at events of almost thirty years earlier. Like Thomas in "Memories of Christmas," (NR 1, SE 1) Angelou, using adult language, maintains the perspective of a twelve-year-old. Students may need to be reminded of events between 1940 and 1969, notably the Supreme Court's school desegregation decision of 1954 that abolished "separate but equal" black and white schools in places like Stamps. One argument against segregated education was that it disadvantaged black children. Although the mature Angelou's sense of being disadvantaged undoubtedly differed from that of the young Angelou, in "Graduation" she re-creates the sense of her young self.

Analytical Considerations

1. You might ask students to examine the pacing of "Graduation" and even diagram the relation of "real" to "fictional" time. How can we measure "real" time? How can we measure "fictional" time?

2. What information does "Graduation" offer about the elementary-school education of black students in Stamps? To what extent was it vocational? To what extent were they "tracked"?

Suggested Writing Assignments

1. Write a retrospective account of an important event in your own life when you were young. Use adult language, maintain the perspective of a child, and manipulate "real" and "fictional" time.
2. Write an argumentative essay against segregated education in the United States using the content of Angelou's narrative to illustrate and support your points.
3. Researchers have posited something called the "Pygmalion effect": Students perform according to what is expected of them, ordinarily by teachers. Do library research on the experiments that led to the name and, using them, write an essay in which you analyze the various expectations the children in Angelou's "Graduation" encountered and what you take to be their effects.

BRUNO BETTELHEIM

A Victim

The Norton Reader, p. 29; Shorter Edition, p. 21

"A Victim" is an excerpt from Bruno Bettelheim's account of his experience in a German concentration camp during World War II, *The Informed Heart: Autonomy in a Mass Age* (1960). It is, explicitly, a flashback: Bettelheim, a psychologist, recollects an event that occurred more than twenty years earlier. Students should notice that Bettelheim uses the event at the clinic to illustrate a point about relations between victims and persecutors and that he adopts a structure of point, illustration, and elaborated point. His narrative thus functions as both illustration and demonstration.

The excerpt is brief. Nevertheless, Bettelheim narrates the event at the clinic with some density and specificity to win our assent, to convince us that, yes, it could indeed happen this way. He does not re-create the event with the density and specificity of other authors in this section who shape events for thematic and emotional resonance, but he does not reduce it to "mere" illustration. Students need to see what Bettelheim does as relevant to their writing, to ask (of themselves) what is enough and what is too much. Bettelheim's narrative engages in its own right, above and beyond the uses to which he puts it, and it is successful because it is, so to speak, excessive.

Analytical Considerations

1. You might ask students to consider Bettelheim's three-part structure of point, illustration, and elaborated point. How does his announcing of his point in advance of the illustration change our reading of it? How would we read it if he withheld his point until later? How does the illustration permit and/or require him to elaborate (and qualify) his point?

2. You might ask students to look at "A Victim" in connection with one or more of the following: Dylan Thomas, "Memories of Christmas" (NR 1, SE 1); Margaret Laurence, "Where the World Began" (NR 6, SE 6); and Maya Angelou, "Graduation" (NR 19, SE 11). Two points of comparison come to mind: the first, differences beween narrative as exploration and narrative as illustration; and the second, differences between flashbacks from adult to child (as in Thomas, Laurence, and Angelou) and from adult to adult (as in Bettelheim).

3. Bettelheim begins "A Victim" by making a large generalization about victims and persecutors. Can his illustration bear the weight of demonstrating it? Or does he, in his elaborated point, qualify his generalization? How can the individual case, or individual cases, demonstrate a generalization? Does the weight of such cases vary according to field of study, say, with respect to literature, social science, and natural science?

Suggested Writing Assignments

1. Write an essay using Bettelheim's three-part structure. Take an experience, present it as an illustration and, insofar as possible, a demonstration.

2. Write two or even three variations on the same event, using Bettelheim's three-part structure and two two-part structures, one of illustration followed by point, the other of point followed by illustration. Then write a paragraph of comment on the various structures and whether you shaped your illustration, or should have shaped your illustration differently in each variation. (First drafts of these essays should probably be discussed in groups.)

JOAN DIDION

On Going Home

The Norton Reader, p. 31; Shorter Edition, p. 23

In a short essay (of six paragraphs) Joan Didion describes returning to her family's home to celebrate her daughter's first birthday. Her husband remains in Los Angeles; she reenters the world of her father, mother, brother, and great-aunts. "On Going Home" proceeds by association: One experience reminds her of another, one question leads to another. What is "home"? Can you go home again? How does memory work? Didion's essay links past and present by shifting incessantly back and forth between them.

Analytical Considerations

1. How does the "vital although troublesome distinction" between *home* as the place where Didion lives with her husband and baby in Los Angeles and *home* as the place where her family lives in the Central Valley of California thread through "On Going Home"?
2. You might want students to look closely at "On Going Home" as an essay developed by association and, in particular, at how Didion maintains the illusion of free association while behaving responsibly toward her readers. She is careful to do two things: to let us know where she is, particularly with respect to present and past, and to provide thematic coherence. For the first, you might ask students to look at transitions between paragraphs and then within them; for the second, to elucidate the several concerns that run through the essay.
3. You might look at "On Keeping a Notebook" (NR 68, SE 490) in conjunction with "On Going Home" with respect to their development and rhetorical techniques. How do objects function in them? How do images function?
4. Consider the titles of both essays—"*On Keeping* a Notebook," "*On Going* Home." What does *on* followed by a participle serve to suggest about the kind of essay each will be?

Suggested Writing Assignments

1. Write a personal essay developed by associations radiating out from a return to a place. Give it a title beginning with *on* followed by a participle.
2. One technique useful to Didion is organizing her associations around objects. Write a personal essay in which you focus on objects. Attend to maintaining the illusion of free association while providing thematic coherence.
3. Write an essay comparing Didion's experience of returning to her family with that of Joyce Maynard in "Four Generations" (NR 38, SE 26).

Additional questions on this essay will be found in the text (NR 34, SE 25–26).

JOYCE MAYNARD

Four Generations

The Norton Reader, p. 38; Shorter Edition, p. 26

In "Four Generations," a visit to her dying grandmother leads Joyce Maynard to consider her familial connections, particularly connections among four generations of women. There are conflicts and frustrations in all such connections, what Joan Didion calls, in "On Going Home" (NR 31, SE 23), "the ambushes of family life." But Maynard comes to see what is stronger: the bonds between generations and the family rituals that provide comfort and security. For another perspective on these bonds see her mother Fredelle Maynard's "And Therefore I Have Sailed the Seas . . ." (NR 38, SE 29).

This essay, like three others—Gloria Naylor's "'Mommy, What Does 'Nigger' Mean?" (NR 378, SE 227), Nancy Mairs' "Who Are You?" (NR 392, SE 247), and Letty Cottin Pogrebin's "It Still Takes a Bride and Groom" (NR 532)—first appeared in the "Hers" column of the *New York Times*. Because they are short (approximately 1,000 words), they are felicitous examples for student writing. Their authors make their points succinctly and choose their illustrations carefully. You will want students to notice how, within the confines of a chronological narrative that begins with her mother's phone call and ends with a stopover in Toronto after she has taken her daughter to visit her grandmother, Maynard provides flashbacks. She opts, however, for full presentation of central incidents and relies on suggestion for their replication from generation to generation. This essay exemplifies something that students need to learn: that a lot about one thing suggests more than a (repetitive) little about a lot of things.

Analytical Considerations

1. How does Maynard characterize each of the four generations? What does she tell readers, what does she imply and leave them to piece together?
2. The death of a loved one can result in a sentimental, overdone account or a stiff-upper-lipped one, or something in between. How would you characterize Maynard's? What feelings does she include, and how does she include them?

Suggested Writing Assignments

1. Maynard focuses on mothers and daughters, not parents and children, and posits a particularly intense relationship between them. Do you think she is correct? Write an essay in which you explore parent-child relationships in your own family, or in some other family you know well, in response to Maynard's exploration of them.
2. After reading Fredelle Maynard's "And Therefore I Have Sailed the Seas . . . ," rewrite Joyce Maynard's "Four Generations" following the daughter's choice and arrangement of incidents but from the mother's perspective and with observations appropriate to her.
3. Write an essay comparing Didion's experience of returning to her family with that of Joyce Maynard in "Four Generations."

Additional questions on this essay will be found in the text (NR 37–38, SE 29).

FREDELLE MAYNARD

And Therefore I Have Sailed the Seas ...

The Norton Reader, p. 38; Shorter Edition, p. 29

The late Fredelle Maynard, Joyce Maynard's mother, published on a range of subjects in popular and literary magazines; "And Therefore I Have Sailed the Seas ..." comes from a collection called *The Tree of Life* published in 1988. In it she repeats some of the intergenerational material that appears in her daughter's "Four Generations" (NR 38, SE 26) and adds to it. She writes about herself and her family, however, with different interests and themes in mind and consequently re-creates them with different emphases. Her essay is about growing old, more specifically, about growing old as a woman. She nevertheless finds it difficult to accept changes that please her as evidence of age: The woman in her sixties still sees herself as "a young girl inexplicably trapped in that body I glimpse as I pass reflecting windows" (paragraph 6).

Fredelle Maynard's essay is longer than Joyce Maynard's, with extended autobiographical passages and extended reflections. Much of her material is organized by comparison: something from the past measured against something from the present, something from the present against something from the past. Many of them involve mothering and grandmothering: Fredelle Maynard, although freer to pursue her own activities, remains enmeshed in the bonds between generations that provide her and her daughter with comfort and security.

Analytical Considerations

1. Maynard's essay bears comparison with E. B. White's "Once More to the Lake" (NR 55, SE 47). White's essay, like hers, involves growing old in an intergenerational context. But her experience seems more determined by gender, or rather, the gendered experience in her essay makes us recognize its absence in his. You might ask students to name these presences and absences and consider how they color each essay.

2. Competitiveness is often regarded as a masculine trait. How does Maynard account for her acquisition of it, and how did she manifest it? What enabled her to become less competitive?

3. Fredelle Maynard's mother and Joyce Maynard's grandmother was a Russian-Jewish immigrant. How does each see her immigrant experience influencing the bonds among generations?

Suggested Writing Assignments

1. Fredelle Maynard recognizes changes in herself and in her circumstances over time without recognizing, at least not with the same force, that she has aged. Does Maynard's separation of the two seem true to your experience? Write an essay in which you consider how old you think you are and how you measure your own age.
2. Read Joyce Maynard's "Four Generations and rewrite it following the daughter's choice and arrangement of incidents but from the mother's perspective and with observations appropriate to her.
3. Read Gloria Steinem's "The Good News Is: These Are Not the Best Years of Your Life" (NR 515, SE 313) with attention to her argument that older women are more actively feminist than younger women. Does her explanation correspond to Maynard's account of her life? Write an essay in which you analyze what Maynard and Steinem have in common, where they diverge, and why.

Additional questions on this essay will be found in the text (NR 48, SE 39–40).

LOREN EISELEY

The Brown Wasps

The Norton Reader, p. 49; Shorter Edition, p. 40

The late Loren Eiseley was an anthropologist, an historian of science, a nature writer, and a poet. "The Brown Wasps" gestures toward nature writing in its title, and wasps, field mice, and pigeons, along with humans, appear in it. What humans share with such animals is a profound attachment to place. Eiseley develops "The Brown Wasps" by association of a particular sort, namely, analogy. By the time students have read his central vignettes—the field mouse or mice who burrowed in his flowerpot, the pigeons who hovered about the steelwork of the old El, and the man, himself, who traveled 2,000 miles to find the tree he and his father had planted—they should grasp how analogy links them.

The first section is somewhat puzzling: Is Eiseley writing about the old men in the railroad station for whom the wasps are a metaphor or the titular wasps for whom the old men are a metaphor? Neither, it turns out, but both. Humans and animals are related by their attachment to place and the support and consolation it affords them.

Eiseley's recourse to analogy leaves the meanings of "The Brown Wasps" to some extent open. Does analogy level humans and animals or open up differences between them? More specifically, does the analogy between the old men in the station and the brown wasps diminish the pathos of the humans or bestow pathos on the wasps? Is Eiseley's return to home as instinctive as that of the (faintly comic) mice digging in his flowerpot and the pigeons circling the deserted El? Or less instinctive than the return of the (somewhat) pathetic mice and pigeons, because he understands what has happened in ways that they do not? Or is it both? Students, ordinarily impatient with ambiguity, may see some virtue, in this essay, of Eiseley's having it both ways.

Analytical Considerations

1. Students should take some time over Eiseley's keen observation and his power to render what he sees in words. You might divide up the essay according to what Eiseley observes and have groups of students work on its various sections and report on them.
2. You might ask students to assess anthropomorphic elements in the language that Eiseley uses to describe wasps, field mice, and pigeons. And the reverse, the language of animal observation that he uses to describe humans.
3. Eiseley's anthropomorphizing language can be compared with Niko Tinbergen's in "The Bee-Hunters of Hulshorst (NR 953, SE 585). What effect does such language achieve?
4. Look at this sentence in Eiseley's final paragraph: "I spoke for myself, one field mouse, and several pigeons" How are we to take it?

Suggested Writing Assignments

1. On the basis of your observation of a particular animal or group of animals, write an essay involving analogy with humans. Think carefully about how you want to use the analogy: to level humans, aggrandize animals, or keep the two in an unstable relation.

2. Write an essay about returning to a place that has disappeared or changed.
3. Write an essay in which you amplify Eiseley's remark: "It is the place that matters, the place at the heart of things" (paragraph 7). You may rely on personal experience alone or on experience, observation, and reading.
4. Write an essay in which you consider "The Brown Wasps" in conjunction with E. B. White's "Once More to the Lake" (NR 55, SE 47) as a meditation on last things. You may want to make this essay a formal comparison.

Additional questions on this essay will be found in the text (NR 55, SE 46–47).

E. B. WHITE

Once More to the Lake

The Norton Reader, p. 55; Shorter Edition, p. 47

"Once More to the Lake" is a classic essay on revisiting the past. With his son E. B. White revisits the lake where he went as a child, and his account, shifting between present and past, measures the passage of time. Generations blur: As White sees his younger self in his son, so he sees his father in his present self. The final sentence—"As he [White's son] buckled the swollen belt suddenly my groin felt the chill of death"—may startle on first reading, but on reflection, White prepares for it. His narrative spans a natural cycle of life passing from one generation to the next; his rendering of natural landscape and pleasurable activity keeps the somber potential meanings of the cycle in the background until, at the very end, he foregrounds them.

In "Once More to the Lake," White combines particular and composite narrative. The particular narrative takes place in the present: White and his son return to the lake on a single occasion. The composite narrative takes place in the past: White recollects repeated episodes from the Augusts he vacationed at the lake. He moves easily but clearly back and forth in time. You might have students notice the shifts in the first paragraph: "One summer, along about 1904," "summer after summer," "A few weeks ago." These references mark transitions fluently, without emphatic breaks. You might ask students to continue noticing how White marks them.

Analytical Considerations

1. How important is White's son to "Once More to the Lake"? How does his presence heighten the passage of time and the theme of mortality? You might ask students to imagine the essay without him.
2. Comparison is an important device in this essay as White again and again balances details from the past against details from the present. Sometimes things change, sometimes they don't. You might ask students which comparisons they remember and then ask them to reread the essay looking for additional ones.
3. Discuss what White reveals about himself (or his persona, his created self) in "Once More to the Lake." Ask what in the text enables us to construct an image of the author.
4. "Once More to the Lake" reveals familiar aspects of E. B. White— see also "Progress and Change" (NR 437, SE 280), "Democracy" (NR 934, SE 572), and "Some Remarks on Humor" (NR 1132). Yet it differs from these other essays as well. You might ask students how in expected or unexpected ways? How are the differences evidence of White's range and flexibility?
5. White's essay bears comparison with Fredelle Maynard's "And Therefore I Have Sailed the Seas . . . " (NR 38, SE 29). Although Maynard's essay, like his, involves growing old in an intergenerational context, her experience seems more determined by gender, or rather, the gendered experience in her essay makes us recognize its absence in his. You might ask students to name these presences and absences and consider how they color each essay.

Suggested Writing Assignments

1. Write an essay about revisiting a place you cherished as a child. Where does "change" lie? In the place? In you? Did the experience lead you to sober reflection on big issues? If so, structure your essay so that you can include reflection as well as narrative and description.
2. Write an essay in which you move retrospectively from the present to the past, drawing specific comparisons between them. Make your thematic emphasis *loss* through the passing of time.
3. Write an essay in which you move retrospectively from the present

to the past drawing specific comparisons between them. Make your thematic emphasis *gain* through the passing of time.

Additional questions on this essay will be found in the text (NR 61, SE 52)

ANATOLE BROYARD

Intoxicated by My Illness

The Norton Reader, p. 61; Shorter Edition, p. 53

Anatole Broyard's "Intoxicated by My Illness" was written for the "His" column of the *New York Times,* which parallels the "Hers" column (see Joyce Maynard, "Four Generations," NR 38, SE 26). These columns are short, approximately 1,000 words, and their authors combine succinct points with telling illustration. Broyard's most telling illustrations, from the title on, are metaphoric: as he observes, "the sick man sees everything as metaphor." Frequently his metaphors are paired; invariably they are surprising, even joking. You will probably need to explain a metaphor like "my existence . . . had taken on a kind of meter, as in poetry, or in taxis" (paragraph 1). Students will be able to explain one like "I now feel as concentrated as a diamond, or a microchip" (paragraph 4). Equally to the point, how do these metaphors characterize Broyard and his response to his illness? How does he intend readers to take them, and do they? "Intoxicated by My Illness" is risk taking: Broyard, choosing to emphasize the unexpected dimensions of what will be a terminal illness, risks straining after novelty, presenting himself as a smart-ass. Student responses to "Intoxicated by My Illness" will probably vary and demonstrate the difficulties Broyard invited by writing it this way. Are some subjects such as grave illness in and of themselves risk taking?

Analytical Considerations

1. You might have students, probably in groups, mark all of Broyard's metaphors and consider the way they work. Are they similar in their surprise, "metaphysical" (as we speak of Donne and other

metaphysical poets) in their wit?
2. Ask students to look at paragraph 14, in which Broyard details the physical effects of his illness. What is literal, what metaphoric?
3. "Intoxicated by My Illness" was published in November 1989; Broyard died about a year later. You might ask students whether knowing of his death changes their reading, and how? (Does it change your own reading?)

Suggested Writing Assignments

1. Experiment with writing an essay on a single subject developed with frequent metaphors. Try to explore unexpected dimensions of the subject and use metaphors that surprise. You might add a paragraph of comment on what these metaphors suggest about you. (In addition, students, in groups, might comment on each other's essays.)
2. Take a subject you think is in and of itself risk taking and write two brief essays on it, one in which you try to avoid risk, and the other in which you calculatedly invite it.
3. Write an essay comparing Broyard's attitudes toward his own mortality with E. B. White's toward his in "Once More to the Lake" (NR 55, SE 47).

PEOPLE, PLACES

ANNIE DILLARD

Terwilliger Bunts One

The Norton Reader, p. 147; Shorter Edition, p. 56

Taken from Dillard's autobiographical *An American Childhood* (1987), this selection might as readily have been titled "My Mother" as anything else, for in it Dillard attempts to characterize her mother— with all her amusing idiosyncrasies and annoying quirks, her remarkable strengths and forgivable weaknesses. Because Dillard depicts a person she knows well, her essay might be compared with Virginia Woolf's "My Father: Leslie Stephen" (NR 134, SE 70) or Doris Lessing's "My Father" (NR 140, SE 62) to raise questions about how a writer conveys a familiar subject to an audience unfamiliar with the subject (through anecdotes rather than adjectives, through the subject's favorite phrases as much as the writer's own words). In contrast, you might use David McCullough's "The Unexpected Mrs. Stowe" (NR 103) or Daniel Epstein's essay about Harry Houdini (NR 122) to ask about the similar and different techniques needed to characterize someone famous whom the writer has never met.

Analytical Considerations

1. You might ask students what anecdotes they remember best about Dillard's mother, why they remember them, and what the anecdotes reveal about the mother's personality.
2. Dillard's mother has many personal qualities her daughter admires: What are those qualities? Does she have qualities about which Dillard is ambivalent? How does Dillard convey her attitude?
3. Dillard's mother lived during a time when the possibilities for women were more limited than they are now, yet Dillard never belabors this point. She simply says, "Mother's energy and intelligence suited her for a greater role in a larger arena—mayor of New York, say—than the one she had" (paragraph 26). Why does Dillard work implicitly rather than explicitly? How does she make her point through examples and anecdotes?
4. This essay is constructed as a series of vignettes, each a page or two long. How does Dillard construct a single vignette? (You might

compare the first with the last.) What organization does Dillard give to the series of vignettes—e.g., why does she begin as she does and end where she ends?

Suggested Writing Assignments

1. Write a character sketch about your mother or some other family member, using techniques from Dillard that you found particularly effective.
2. "Torpid conformity was a kind of sin; it was stupidity itself" (paragraph 32), according to Dillard's mother. Write an essay in which you illustrate this thesis with examples from your own experience.
3. Take a phrase or common saying from your own family's history. Write a brief essay in which you convey what that phrase or saying means to you and your family.

DORIS LESSING

My Father

The Norton Reader, p. 140; Shorter Edition, p. 62

Doris Lessing's "My Father" can be compared with two other character sketches in this section—Virginia Woolf's "My Father: Leslie Stephen" (NR 134, SE 70) and Annie Dillard's "Terwilliger Bunts One" (NR 147, SE 56)—with the goal of seeing similarities and differences in approach. A comparison of Lessing and Woolf should be of special interest because of the similarities of the authors. Both Lessing and Woolf are modern novelists (Lessing is contemporary), and both are daughters of British fathers who had unusual adventures outside England. Both authors seem to wish to render true portraits of their fathers: Woolf points out peccadilloes as well as gemlike qualities in Leslie Stephen; Lessing begins by announcing the difficult task she is undertaking of writing a "true" account of Alfred Cook.

Doris Lessing's attempt to write a "true" description of her father results in a maturely and sensitively executed character portrait. Lessing is thorough and successful in her efforts to describe her father objectively: She looks into records, considers the views of others who knew him, quotes statements made by her father, and accepts the responsibility of critically evaluating him. Complete objectivity and definition are impossible, however—first, because the author's close personal relation to her subject makes her necessarily somewhat subjective and, second, because a human being can never be wholly delineated. Perhaps such limitations finally enrich the essay, for they make Lessing's character portrait all the more human.

Analytical Considerations

1. The essay opens with a striking simile, "We use our parents like recurring dreams." Scrutinize the text for recurrences of the word *dream* and for the presence of related words like *nightmare*. How does repetition work both rhetorically and thematically? In what sense might this essay be called a "dream sequence"?

2. Direct attention to the principles of development in the essay. Lessing builds her essay with particular blocks of material. Focus on her use of specific devices—e.g., photographs, quotations, anecdotes, memories—and determine what they contribute to the whole. Consider the architectural design of the whole essay.

3. Is there a single dominant impression Lessing wishes to create about her father? Where in the text is she most effective in trying to create that impression?

4. Re: voice. In the opening paragraph Lessing begins with the first-person plural pronoun *we*, then shifts to three uses of the first-person singular pronoun (*me, I, my*). Ask students how this pronoun shift functions. It reveals an integral element of Lessing's rhetorical strategy: her attempt to establish a shared purpose and identity with her readers. Is she successful in drawing the reader into the process of this essay?

5. At least in certain areas, Lessing strikes a stance of objectivity, and it is useful to ask not only *how* but *why*. What "distancing techniques" does she use? You might point out, for example, how in paragraph 22 the narrator "unobtrusively" shifts emphasis from the objective to the subjective. Ask students how objective Lessing is and whether or not complete objectivity is possible, or even desirable, in an essay like this.

6. What is the purpose of this essay? Is it a memorial in words? An exorcism? A simple reminiscence? An attempt at definition or self-definition?

7. One of the important aspects of this essay has to do with hiding and revealing. Notice that Lessing tells us her father grew a mustache to hide "a heavily-jutting upper lip" (paragraph 2); later (paragraph 8) she speculates that when he changed his handwriting, he may have

"created a new personality for himself." Although it may be fairly easy to determine what Lessing has consciously revealed in "My Father," it may not be so easy to determine what she has hidden. Nonetheless, it is important to direct attention to absences as well as presences. Ask students what is missing. Discuss whether or not Lessing has unconsciously revealed more than she may have intended.

8. This essay was reprinted in an abridged form in *Vogue* (Feb. 15, 1964) under the title "All Seething Underneath." Students might be asked to find the source for that title (paragraph 19), establish its context, and evaluate its appropriateness. Such a discussion gives attention to an often-neglected aspect of an essay: its title.

9. This essay is pervaded by bittersweet nostalgia ("I knew him when his best years were over," paragraph 1). Woolf's essay has something of the same tone ("By the time that his children were growing up, the great days of my father's life were over," paragraph 1). Encourage students to explore both essays to determine how tone is generated and sustained.

10. "My Father" needs to be read as a cultural document, a text through which a certain culture speaks. Prompt students to think about this perspective by asking what the essay reveals about colonialism, racism, sexism, and imperialism.

Suggested Writing Assignments

1. Lessing pays considerable attention to her father's traumatic experience in World War I; she notes that "the best of my father died in that war" (paragraph 13). Write an essay about what the experience of war has done to someone you know.

2. One of the interesting absences in Lessing's essay is her mother. Although she is mentioned at seven points (paragraphs 3, 20, 21, 24, 26, 28, 33), and thus is technically "present," what is the status of the mother's presence? How much do we learn? Write a biographical essay on Lessing's mother, using just the material culled from "My Father."

3. Read Lessing's essay titled "Impertinent Daughters," written more than twenty years after "My Father." It appeared in *Granta* (no. 14, winter 1984). Write an essay comparing and contrasting not only Lessing's attitudes toward her parents but the ways in which she has expressed those attitudes. Can you draw any conclusions about Lessing's development as a person? As an artist?

4. Obtain the text of "All Seething Underneath." Examine it to

determine where and how "My Father" was abridged (and by whom). Write an essay in which you consider differences in purpose and audience between these two versions. Which is the more effective essay? Why?

5. Write an essay, based on actual experience, that illustrates "how a man's (woman's) good qualities can also be his (her) bad ones or, if not bad, a danger to him (her)."

Additional questions on this essay will be found in the text (NR 147, SE 69).

VIRGINIA WOOLF

My Father: Leslie Stephen

The Norton Reader, p. 134; Shorter Edition, p. 70

Virginia Woolf, one of the finest novelists and literary critics of the twentieth century, was an acute reader and renderer of character. In this portrait of her father, a great thinker and author in his own right, Woolf is able to bring the man to life. But we are certainly (and perhaps naturally) given a biased view of Leslie Stephen. Try as she might to leaven her praise with honest evaluation, the admiring daughter creates a glowing portrait of her father as a paragon of men. Perhaps Stephen was a paragon, a model scholar, father, and friend, but some students may feel that Woolf's portrait is a little too perfect. You might ask them to compare it with Doris Lessing's portrait of her father, to discuss the different purposes of these essays, and to suggest how different purposes may have led the two writers to alternate approaches to biography.

For instructors using *The Norton Reader* a comparison of Woolf's portrait of her father with her character sketch of Ellen Terry (NR 116) might lead to a useful discussion of how one writes about a familiar subject versus how one describes a famous, public personage. Woolf's "Ellen Terry" begins with a memory of the great actress on the stage of the Court Theatre, but essentially is constructed from the details of Terry's own memoirs, *Story of My Life*. You might ask how the examples and anecdotes in the two biographical portraits differ, as well as how the structures of the essays differ, with "My Father: Leslie Stephen" organizing itself around character traits and "Ellen Terry" following a chronological pattern.

Analytical Considerations

1. Examine the text of the essay for clues to Woolf's purpose in writing "My Father: Leslie Stephen." Direct attention to the original context of the essay—that of Woolf writing her recollections for a general readership. In addition to Woolf's public purposes in writing, you might raise the idea that Woolf was writing for herself as a means of understanding her relationship with her father.

2. We know the audience for the original publication of this essay consisted of readers of the London *Times* of London on November 28, 1932. (Stephen died in 1904, so this essay first appeared twenty-eight years after his death). Ask students to look for textual clues that reveal Woolf's awareness of her audience, e.g., "Even today there may be parents" (paragraph 10).

3. Examine the design of the essay. Does it use chronology as an ordering mechanism? Does it organize details around abstract qualities that are taken up one by one? Does it use some other principle of organization? Study and label what each paragraph does in the development of the essay. If you have read Dillard's essay "Terwilliger Bunts One" (NR 147, SE 56), you might compare and contrast her mode of organization with Woolf's.

4. Good description often coalesces around a dominant impression. Discuss the dominant impression Woolf creates about her father and how she creates it. Ask students to be specific about assertions and kinds of support (anecdote, quotation, memory, etc.). Distinguish between the use and value of fairly "objective" information (the testimony of others; Stephen's remarks) and the use and value of fairly "subjective" material (Woolf's own memories and opinions).

5. What persona emerges from "My Father: Leslie Stephen"? Walker Gibson, *Persona: A Style Study for Readers and Writers* (New York: Random House, 1969), is a useful resource for this type of analysis. Students could benefit from a one-page summary with examples from Gibson; although he deals exclusively with fiction, his comments also apply to nonfiction.

6. In paragraph 4, Woolf describes her father's habit of drawing beasts on the flyleaves of his books and scribbling pungent analyses in the margins; then she notes that these "brief comments" were the "germ of the more temperate statements of his essays." This aptly illustrates the process of composition for many of us. Encourage students to see that reading offers possibilities for establishing a dialogue between writer and reader, that careful reading involves

annotation. You might devote some class discussion to fostering this sense of involvement with the text.

7. Woolf reveals, perhaps unconsciously, some rather unpleasant and dislikable aspects of her father here. Do such elements belong in a biographical sketch? From what you have read do you believe that Leslie Stephen was the "most lovable of men" (paragraph 11)?

8. When Woolf says of Leslie Stephen, "The things that he did not say were always there in the background" (paragraph 5) and "Too much, perhaps, has been said of his silence" (paragraph 7), she directs our attention to an oft-neglected dimension of the text: silences and absences. Ask students to reconstruct the image of Leslie Stephen based on the information Woolf leaves out of her essay.

9. Woolf says of her father that "when he described a person . . . he would convey exactly what he thought of him in two or three words" (paragraph 5). Let students try this exercise on Woolf, on Stephen, or on a fellow student.

Suggested Writing Assignments

1. Write a character sketch of a parent or grandparent. Strive for the concreteness and balance that Woolf has worked toward in "My Father: Leslie Stephen."

2. Read two or three other biographical sketches by Woolf (including "Ellen Terry," NR 116). Compare and contrast them on points of subject, purpose, audience, tone, and content.

3. Read Doris Lessing's portrait titled "My Father" (NR 140, SE 62). Is Virginia Woolf better or less able to render an objective picture of her father than Lessing is of hers? If one author is more objective than another, what accounts for that ability? Is it approach or personality? Write an essay comparing and contrasting these two selections.

4. How does Woolf define *fatherhood* in her essay? Using examples from "My Father: Leslie Stephen," write an essay on Woolf's conception of fatherhood.

Additional questions on this essay will be found in the text (NR 139, SE 74-75)

MARGARET MEAD

Home and Travel

The Norton Reader, p. 153; *Shorter Edition*, p. 75

A serious scholar and seminal figure in the relatively new science of anthropology, Margaret Mead was, by the end of her life, a familiar figure to most Americans. Many had read her scientific and theoretical works—*Coming of Age in Samoa* or *Male and Female*, for instance—because she wrote for a lay as well as professional audience. In this respect Mead antedated such contemporary scientist —popular writers as Carl Sagan, Isaac Asimov, Lewis Thomas, Elisabeth Kübler-Ross, and Stephen Jay Gould (all of whom are represented in *The Norton Reader*). Millions of other Americans came to know Mead through her television appearances, in which she applied her studies of other cultures to issues in contemporary American society, managing always to be provocative, if not controversial. Mead's availability to the general public made her an unusual scientist; her life and views made her an unusual woman of her time—an important early feminist.

"Home and Travel" is taken from Mead's autobiographical best-seller *Blackberry Winter* (1972). It is not an anthropological piece, but Mead's research among faraway cultures is reflected in several examples near the end of the essay. As Mead wrote in the acknowledgments to *Blackberry Winter*, "Although the focus . . . is not on [the peoples of her research], they are nonetheless present."

Analytical Considerations

1. You might ask students what kind of essay this is—narrative, descriptive, expository (if so, what kind?), or argumentative—and why they think Mead chooses this form (or these forms).
2. Questions of purpose and audience are relevant here and, because "Home and Travel" comes from an autobiography, could lead to a consideration of what goes into autobiographical writing.
3. You might spend some time examining this essay for patterns of transition between specific examples/episodes and passages of reflection/commentary. Students might consider how these elements function as parts of the whole essay—or, if you have discussed Analytical Consideration 2, why autobiographical writing needs such patterns of transition. Does Mead give rhetorical clues to alert the reader to her shifts (as in paragraph 13)?

4. Ask students to analyze Mead's prose. Choose a paragraph and study her sentences for length, type, variation, and punctuation. Choose another and do the same.
5. Consider "Home and Travel" as a cultural document. What does it say about role definition for women? About the power of cultural forces?
6. Ask students to characterize the persona of the writer of "Home and Travel."

Suggested Writing Assignments

1. Write an essay about what the word *home* means to you. You might clarify your personal meaning by discussing what home means to others, both inside and outside your culture.
2. Compare and contrast Mead's understanding of *home* with that of Joan Didion in "On Going Home" (NR 31, SE 23).
3. Mead was a provocative, often controversial, guest on television talk shows, where she frequently aired her views on contemporary culture and behavior. In the middle section of "Home and Travel" (paragraphs 13, 14, 15), she offers some commentary on "children today." Respond to her analysis with an essay of your own.

Additional questions on this essay will be found in the text (NR 157–58, SE 79).

N. SCOTT MOMADAY

The Way to Rainy Mountain

The Norton Reader, p. 158; Shorter Edition, p. 80

Momaday's description of his grandmother and his return to Rainy Mountain, a place sacred to the Kiowa Indians, employs a structure common to many cultures: that of the journey as an actual and metaphorical quest. You might ask students about their own journeys and journeys they have read about in literature—whether in Homer's *Odyssey* or Jack Kerouac's *On the Road* or some even more recent piece of travel writing. Why do we travel? What do we expect to gain from travel? What did Momaday hope to discover by returning to his grandmother's house and retracing the traditional movements of the Kiowas? Such questions might help students to think about the journey structure as a possible one for their own personal reports or for their descriptions of a place of special interest to them. The journey Momaday describes in "Rainy Mountain" beautifully links realistic descriptions of the West, sacred myths of the Kiowas, and memories of his grandmother and her stories to evoke a sense of the importance of place in his own individual life.

Analytical Considerations

1. What is the structure of this essay? You might ask students to compare Momaday's actual journey (introduced in paragraph 2 and again in paragraph 5) with the historical journeys of his ancestors, the Kiowas. How are the two journeys linked?
2. Why does Momaday begin and end with descriptions of Rainy Mountain? How and why are the two descriptions different?
3. Where does Momaday include cultural myths, historical events, or his grandmother's stories in this essay? How do these enrich our understanding of the places Momaday revisits?
4. To what extent are "people" essential to our understanding of "place"? Discuss the ways in which Momaday describes his grandmother both as grandmother (i.e., a real person, a family member) and as Kiowa Indian (i.e., a representative of an older culture that no longer exists). Why do we need both views of his grandmother to understand the significance of Momaday's return to his ancestral home?
5. Look closely at sentences in which Momaday chooses words with metaphorical or symbolic significance—e.g., in paragraph 1 where he links Rainy Mountain to the place "where Creation was begun," or in paragraph 5 where he refers to his journey as a "pilgrimage," or in paragraph 9 where he refers to the soldiers stopping of Indian rituals as "deicide." Discuss the connotations of such words and phrases and how they enrich the literal journey that Momaday takes.

Suggested Writing Assignments

1. Write about a journey you took to a place important in your family's history—whether an ancestral home, the home of a relative, or a home you lived in as a child.
2. Write about a place with historical and cultural significance, combining your own observations with history, legend, and/or myth.
3. Write a descriptive essay about a person and place that seem intertwined. In doing so, think about why the person seems so essential to understanding the place.

GRETEL EHRLICH

The Solace of Open Spaces

The Norton Reader, p. 163; Shorter Edition, p. 85

Why are "open spaces" so important to us as North Americans? Gretel Ehrlich, one of our finest contemporary essayists, explores this question in "The Solace of Open Spaces," an essay about Wyoming and her experiences there as a rancher. Ehrlich tells us that she went to Wyoming to find "the numbness I thought I wanted," but that she found something better, a "vitality," a new life. Ehrlich suggests that Americans need to reconsider their relation to space; instead of building "*against* space," we need to learn that space "can heal what is divided and burdensome in us." This essay, like Momaday's "Way to Rainy Mountain" (NR 158, SE 80) can provide students with an opportunity to understand not only *how* to write about places but *why* such writing is important within our culture.

"The Solace of Open Spaces" might be compared with Ehrlich's "Spring,"(N 574 SE 356) included in "Nature and the Environment," to show how a writer can use the same kinds of materials for different purposes. Both "Open Spaces" and "Spring" are set in Wyoming, both occur during spring, both emerge from the writer's personal experience. Yet this essay focuses on Wyoming itself, its personal and cultural significance, whereas "Spring" focuses on the season, its meaning as a recurring, cyclical pattern in human and natural life.

Analytical Considerations

1. How does a writer describe a "place" as big as Wyoming? You might ask students to list the various materials—facts, statistics, history, legends, personal experiences, and conversations—that Ehrlich includes in this essay.
2. Analyze a paragraph in which "research" underlies description— e.g., paragraph 4 in which Ehrlich describes the Big Horn Mountains not as they appear today but as they have been shaped by geological forces. You might ask students to try a similar paragraph of description, using a place they might later choose for a full essay.
3. Where does Ehrlich use statistics? Where does she use metaphorical language? Why do both often appear within the same paragraph? How do both contribute to our understanding of Wyoming?
4. This essay uses a series of small sections (almost mini-essays) as its

mode of organization. You might ask students to analyze one (or more) of these sections, how it begins and ends, what it contains, why it appears where it does in the series. Then you might ask what advantages Ehrlich gains from this mode of organization—as compared, for example, with Momaday's use of the journey to organize his essay.

5. Why does Ehrlich explain her reasons for coming to Wyoming where she does (paragraph 8)? Why does she save her comments on Wyoming's significance for modern human beings until the end of the essay?

Suggested Writing Assignments

1. Write an essay about the state you now live in or a state which you know well, using the same combination of personal experience, collected stories, and research that Ehrlich does.
2. Choose a section from "The Solace of Open Spaces" that appeals to you, and use it as a model for your own mini-essay about a place.
3. Compare and contrast "The Solace of Open Spaces" with "Spring." What are the different purposes of the essays? How do these purposes alter the form and content of the essays? Illustrate your points with specific details from both essays.

HUMAN NATURE

DESMOND MORRIS

Territorial Behavior

The Norton Reader, p. 188; Shorter Edition, p. 94

Desmond Morris, trained as a zoologist, became keeper of mammals at the London Zoo (and a well-known guest on television talk shows). "Territorial Behavior" was published in his *Manwatching: A Field Guide to Human Behavior* (1979). The title of the volume should tell students something about Morris' approach. He uses the observational and descriptive strategies of an animal behaviorist and an anthropologist to describe us. Some critics have said that the parallels he draws between humans and animals are reductive, that he emphasizes similarities and neglects differences. Students nevertheless find this essay convincing, not only because of the wealth of illustration he provides but also because it is telling: It matches their experience.

Morris' three-part classificatory scheme provides an almost diagrammatic structure for "Territorial Behavior." Students will undoubtedly notice how Morris uses the scheme, and it's worth considering in conjunction with their own writing. Classificatory schemes are useful heuristics, particularly on examinations, often on short papers. But experienced writers, as *The Norton Reader* attests, do not often use them to provide structures for entire essays, and when they do, as Morris does here, they load them with illustrations to counteract their potential thinness and arbitrariness.

Analytical Considerations

1. Look at Morris' descriptive language. For example, in his (brief) first paragraph—"A territory is a defended space. In the broadest sense, there are three kinds of territory: tribal, family and personal"—*territory* suggests parallels with animals; *tribe,* with aboriginal peoples. In point of fact, because *tribe* is inappropriate to modern nation-states, Morris comes up with the category *pseudo-tribe* (paragraph 8). You might ask students to locate other

examples of diction that suggests zoological and anthropological parallels and consider whether they diminish humans.

2. William Golding also uses a three-part classificatory scheme in "Thinking as a Hobby" (NR 181, SE 118). You might ask students to consider, for both essays, how each author deploys three classes. Morris uses them to distinguish size (large, medium, and small); Golding, rank (first-rate, second-rate, and third-rate). But why three? Why not two or four?

Suggested Writing Assignments

1. Write an essay in which you apply the classifications of territorial behavior developed by Morris to a group of which you are a member and then to specific individuals within it, an intimate group like family or friends or a larger group like a class or a team or a club or students in a dormitory.

2. You can test and, if necessary, modify Morris' description of personal space. Make a list of the characteristics of personal space and the ways people defend it. Systematically (but gently) violate the boundaries of other people's personal space and take notes on their behavior. Decide how to write up the results of your observations—as personal narrative, impersonal report, or a combination of the two—and do it.

3. As Morris finds in humans the behavior of animals, so Carl Sagan, in "The Abstractions of Beasts" (NR 613, SE 392), finds in animals the behavior of humans. Drawing on these two essays, write a speculative essay on drawing (and blurring) the lines between humans and animals.

Additional questions on this essay will be found in the text (NR 264–65, SE 153).

PAUL THEROUX

Being a Man

The Norton Reader, p. 219; Shorter Edition, p. 102

Paul Theroux is a novelist, short-story writer, and essayist; "Being a Man" was published in a collection called *Sunrise with Seamonsters*

(1985). Theroux takes a calculatedly strong and unqualified line that is both personal—"I have always disliked being a man" (paragraph 2)—and general—"Any objective study would find the quest for manliness essentially right-wing, puritanical, cowardly, neurotic and fueled largely by a fear of women" (paragraph 7). Midway through the essay he discloses an ax to grind, his desire to be a writer when, in the United States, to write, especially fiction, is considered unmanly. His personal involvement, however, does not lead him to qualify his assertion that the quest for manliness is bad for everybody. It is possible to say that Theroux's strong line is subverted by his involvement. But is it necessary to say so? While academic writing is usually qualified writing, it is only one kind of writing, and its rules are the rules of a specialized discourse.

Analytical Considerations

1. Ask students to mark Theroux's generalizations and consider how he makes them. You might also ask them to rewrite one or two as qualified generalizations.
2. Call attention to Theroux's illustrations. Ordinarily he uses one. The exception is paragraphs 10 and 11, where he surveys a number of writers. What are uses of single and multiple illustrations?

Suggested Writing Assignments

1. Write an essay in which you take a strong, unqualified position on a subject with which you are personally involved.
2. Do library research on one or more of the writers Theroux mentions in paragraphs 10 and 11. Write an essay in which you test his assertion that the quest for manliness is particularly destructive for writers. In qualifying his generalization, be careful to qualify your own.
3. Both Paul Theroux and Herb Goldberg, in "In Harness: The Male Condition" (NR 509, SE 307), look at the condition of being a man, one with personal engagement, the other with clinical detachment. Write an essay in which you consider the advantages and disadvantages of each strategy.

Additional questions on this essay will be found in the text (NR 222, SE 105–06).

SCOTT RUSSELL SANDERS

Looking at Women

The Norton Reader, p. 222; Shorter Edition, p. 106

Scott Russell Sanders tells us in the course of "Looking at Women" that he was eleven when he saw the girl in the pink shorts and that, thirty years later, he is married and the father of two; his wife's name is Ruth. If we are interested in him as an author as well as a looker at women, he is also a professor of English at Indiana University (which may explain his quoting the improbable Miss Indiana Persimmon Festival) and has published scholarly works, science fiction, and nonfiction. He has also written an essay on the essay that appears in *The Norton Reader*, "The Singular First Person" (NR 1100, SE 696). In it he talks about the rules for writing an essay he was taught as a schoolboy and his impatience with them: Among them, he lists linear development, that is, thesis sentences and transitions, and avoiding *I*, the "singular first person" of his title (paragraphs 12 to 13). He prefers "dodging and leaping," "the shimmer and play of mind on the surface and in the depths a strong current." He is also fond of metaphor, as when he likens his preferred essay form to a river.

Much of "Looking at Women" is personal report and, if Sanders does not succeed in making his experiences and his perceptions interesting, readers will find it hard going. But the essay is more than personal report. Sanders treats a timely and loaded question: how the gaze, directed at women by men, by construction workers as well as by artists, can reduce them to objects of desire. Through his reminiscences and musings, Sanders looks at men's looking at women and women's being looked at. He wants to exempt himself (and other men like him?) from reducing them to objects, to demonstrate that he views them not as "sexual playthings but as loved persons" (paragraph 31). Because the essay is wide-ranging, Sanders suggests the complexity of male gazes other than his and the complexity of female self-presentation. The responses of students, both male and female, to Sanders' essay should raise questions about making the personal representative, about the *I* as an analytic instrument, both particularized and generalized. Sanders' essay, with its focus on the personal and particular, gestures toward inclusiveness and the general. Sanders' success in combining the particular and the general is an open question, as is, indeed, what we mean when we say a piece of writing is a success.

Analytical Considerations

1. What kind of development does Sanders provide in place of linear development? You might direct students to his "What I present here are a few images and reflections that cling, for me, to this one item" (paragraph 13).
2. What does the pronoun *I* entail for Sanders? How is self-presentation as he uses it both risk taking and self-protective?
3. What kinds of metaphors does Sanders use? To what extent are they subsumed into the essay, to what extent are they showy, calling attention to themselves?
4. Sanders includes in his essay a number of other voices. You might have students list them and notice who speaks for men, who for women. You might also have them notice that Sanders quotes a psychologist, Allen Wheelis, twice, and ask what work the Wheelis quotations do?

Suggested Writing Assignments

1. Write an essay with at least four sections developed by association in which you use, as Sanders puts it, "images and reflections that cling" (paragraph 13). Begin the first section with an incident and return to it in the fourth.
2. Locate and read the *Playboy* interview with Jimmy Carter that Sanders mentions (paragraph 20) and some of the responses to it. Write an essay in which you analyze the interview and the responses. Use *I* in a way that seems appropriate to you. How much of your experience will go into your essay, and how will you include it?
3. Look at Sanders' definition of pornography: "making flesh into a commodity, flaunting it like any other merchandise, divorcing bodies from selves" (paragraph 37). Do some library research on the Supreme Court's definition of pornography. Write an essay in which you contrast Sanders' personal definition with the Supreme Court's general definition.

Additional questions on this essay will be found in the text (NR 233–34, SE 117).

WILLIAM GOLDING

Thinking as a Hobby

The Norton Reader, p. 181; Shorter Edition, p. 118

In this essay, William Golding juxtaposes a three-part classificatory scheme, rather casually introduced, with an autobiographical account of his development, from school to university, in learning what it means to think. "Thinking as a Hobby" may profitably be contrasted with Desmond Morris' "Territorial Behavior" (NR 188, SE 94). Morris provides a serious behavioral analysis for which classification is the appropriate mode of presentation, whereas Golding illustrates his categories with a couple of comic figures each and turns even his encounter with Einstein into comedy. While what passes for thinking—i.e., "grade-three thinking" and "grade-two thinking," is comic, serious thinking—"grade-one thinking"—is not, and an adequate treatment of Einstein would require a major shift in tone.

Incomprehension or being left in the lurch—there I was, not understanding a thing, while everybody else was in on the situation and coping—is a dangerous subject for students: They reproduce in writing broadly comic accounts that come easily to them and probably are funny when they tell them to families and friends. But such accounts may not work as written essays. If your students have been writing this broad kind of humor, you might want them to look at the sharpness and specificity of Golding's comedy. But "Thinking as a Hobby" may not be a good model for all students; few of them are capable of his wry perception and tonal subtlety.

Analytical Considerations

1. How does Golding's title, "Thinking as a Hobby," signal his comic intent? You might ask the same question about his categories: "grade-three thinking," "grade-two thinking," and "grade-one thinking."
2. See Desmond Morris, "Territorial Behavior" Analytical Considerations 2, on three-part classificatory schemes. Golding actually uses two such schemes: three kinds of thinking and three statuettes on the cupboard behind the headmaster's desk. The

second, a "found" scheme rather than a "made" one (at least according to what he tells us in the essay), is more arbitrary than his "made" scheme. What is it and how does he use it?

Suggested Writing Assignments

1. Write a comic account of at least two individuals you know who exemplify Golding's "grade-one thinking" and "grade-two thinking."
2. Writing a serious account of an individual you know or have read about who exemplifies Golding's "grade-three thinking"; you may want to give it another name. You might read the descriptions of Einstein in Jacob Bronowski's "The Nature of Scientific Reasoning" (NR 1008, SE 613) and Horace Freeland Judson's "The Rage to Know" (NR 942, SE 574) and use Einstein as your example.

Additional questions on this essay will be found in the text (NR 187, SE 124).

JACOB BRONOWSKI

The Reach of Imagination

The Norton Reader, p. 125; Shorter Edition, p. 35

The late Jacob Bronowski wrote about both science and literature and was responsible for a television series that you (and some of your students) may have seen, "The Ascent of Man" (1973–74). He held that scientific and poetic thinking are essentially the same, both originating in the imagination and both tested by experience. This essay might be read in conjunction with his "The Nature of Scientific Reasoning" (NR 1008, SE 613); although written for independent publication, the second extends the concept of imagination that appears in the first. In the first, Bronowski defines the imagination by its nature and scope. His illustrations from science and from literature exemplify, affirm similarities between scientific and poetic thinking, and buttress his authority. Students will recognize his magisterial range of illustrations as beyond their resources. What kinds of authority, then, are available to them? Many kinds, it's important to emphasize, so long as they moderate their claims to pronounce on large issues, stake out smaller ones, and deploy the authority of others without losing their personal voice. You might consider requiring Suggested Writing Assignment 2 and using successful and less successful student papers to illustrate the problematics of authority.

Analytical Considerations

1. *"To imagine,"* according to Bronowski, "means to make images and to move them about inside one's head in new arrangements" (paragraph 9). Ask students to trace the ways Bronowski enlarges this definition through illustration.
2. You might have students list Bronowski's illustrations and references, perhaps in two columns, labeled science and literature. Which illustrations does he explain, which does he simply refer to? What do his illustrations and references suggest about his intended audience?

Suggested Writing Assignments

1. Write an essay in which you imitate, on a smaller scale, Bronowski's procedures. Take the simplest definition available (in a dictionary) of some abstract term of your choosing. Extend it with at least three illustrations, one of which is drawn from personal experience, another from an authority.
2. "Imagination," Bronowski claims, "is a specifically *human* gift." (paragraph 1). Argue against or qualify his claim. Draw your evidence from and buttress your own authority with other authorities by using one or more of the following essays: David Rains Wallace, "The Mind of the Beaver" (NR 606, SE 365); Konrad Z. Lorenz, "The Taming of the Shrew" (NR 588, SE 374); Carl Sagan, "The Abstractions of Beasts" (NR 613, SE 392); and Niko Tinbergen, "The Bee-Hunters of Hulshorst" (NR 953, SE 585). While you use the voices (and the authority) of Wallace, Lorenz, Sagan, or Tinbergen through quotation, don't let their voices (and authority) drown out yours.
3. In conjunction with Analytical Consideration 2, read another essay in Bronowski's *Science and Human Values* (1956, 1965) and, using it, "The Reach of Imagination," and his prefatory material, write an essay in which you reconstruct Bronowski's sense of audience and purpose in this volume. Be sure to display your evidence and account for your interpretation of it.

Additional questions on this essay will be found in the text (NR 203, SE 132).

M. F. K. FISHER

Moment of Wisdom

The Norton Reader, p. 205; Shorter Edition, p. 132

M. F. K. Fisher—she always uses her initials—is Mary Frances Kennedy Fisher. She is known as a writer on food, which is to say that in her autobiographical reminiscences of home —Whittier, California—and abroad Europe, where she has traveled and lived— eating is a thematic and associative device as well as a subject. This essay comes from a collection about growing old, *Sister Age,* published in 1983. Students will see the way it is put together, with introductory and concluding generalizations about the tears that signify wisdom— "simmered, boiled, sieved, filtered past all anger and into the realm of acceptive serenity" (paragraph 15)—framing two illustrative vignettes, one extensive, one brief. These are not the usual illustrations of expository and argumentative prose. The first describes a scene inclusively and suggestively; Fisher renders both more and less than we need to know to understand her tears. Her illustration requires interpretation, much like a short story; in sensibility and technique she may remind us of Katherine Mansfield.

Students will probably have divided opinions on this essay, depending on their responses to Fisher's sensibility and to the careful reading and interpretation she requires of them. You might suggest that her strategy of indirection is warranted by our vocabulary for the direct expression of emotion. To be *moved to tears* generalizes a variety of responses that include tears by reducing them to a single response. Fisher attempts to discriminate tears of wisdom from other kinds of tears by describing them (paragraphs 1 and 15). But it is her rendering of two occasions (the longer rendering in particular) that enables us to inflect her tears of wisdom exactly.

Analytical Considerations

1. You will want to make sure that students, reading Fisher's vignette of Whittier, notice statements to the effect that she was twelve; that crying was not encouraged in her family; that she seldom cried; that her tears surprised her; that her grandmother had recently died, within days; and that she says the death had not bothered her.

2. You will probably want also to look at the immediate occasion of her tears, that is, the frail old man selling Bibles, as well as their larger context.

Suggested Writing Assignments

1. Write an essay about a particular kind of emotional response in which you rely on narration (of one or two incidents) to explain it. Be sure at least to identify the emotion involved and perhaps to discriminate it from other kinds in your opening and closing paragraphs.
2. Read selections from one of Fisher's volumes on food. Examine at least two of her renderings of scene and ambiance and discuss the techniques that warrant her reputation as a writer on food.

LEWIS THOMAS

The Long Habit

The Norton Reader, p. 247; Shorter Edition, p. 136

Two essays in this section discuss the feelings that attend our thinking about death: Lewis Thomas' "The Long Habit" and Elisabeth Kübler-Ross' "On the Fear of Death" (NR 252, SE 140). A third, Stephen Jay Gould's "Our Allotted Lifetimes" (NR 260, SE 148) challenges us to think about death differently. You might assign all three. Thomas' essay, brief and direct, moves between the emotional and medical aspects of dying; Kübler-Ross' looks at dying patients and their needs and rights; Gould's measures our life span against that of other mammals and concludes that we live an exceptionally long time.

Lewis Thomas, trained as a physician, is a former dean of the Yale Medical School and president emeritus of the Memorial Sloan-Kettering Center for Cancer Research. In 1970 he began to write "Notes of a Biology Watcher" for the *New England Journal of Medicine;* these columns, of which "The Long Habit" is an example, have been collected and published in several volumes for a wider audience. Patients, he observes, are not alone in their reluctance to think about dying; doctors have only recently begun to think about it themselves. Thomas has amassed a considerable amount of (necessarily secondhand) information about dying. But his magisterial treatment of it encompasses more than its physiology and psychology. He generalizes easily about *our* attitudes toward life and death. Students cannot expect to claim his authority, but they can consider how, on the one hand, he claims it within the essay, and how, on the other hand, we cede it to him because of who he is and where his essay was published (and republished).

Analytical Considerations

1. You might ask students to mark Thomas' *we*'s and whatever other pronouns he uses. How frequently does he use *we*? Who does *we* signify in his essay? What kind of authority does Thomas claim by his use of *we*? What right does he have to claim it?
2. You might also ask students to notice Thomas' generalizations and consider how they might appropriate them in their own writing. Do they need Thomas' support or can they recast them as their own?
3. Consider what Thomas and Kübler-Ross, in "On the Fear of Death," say about the mechanical prolongation of life.

Suggested Writing Assignments

1. Read Thomas' "On Magic in Medicine" (NR 483, SE 296). Write an essay in which you use the two essays to illustrate and analyze Thomas' views of life and death.
2. Do library research on returning from death, on what Thomas calls the Lazarus syndrome (paragraph 12). Then write an essay in which you describe, evaluate, and also speculate on the information you have discovered.

Additional questions on this essay will be found in the text (NR 251, SE 140).

ELISABETH KÜBLER-ROSS

On the Fear of Death

The Norton Reader, p. 252; Shorter Edition, p. 140

Two essays in this section discuss the feelings that attend our thinking about death: Lewis Thomas' "The Long Habit" (NR 247, SE 136) and Elisabeth Kübler-Ross' "On the Fear of Death." A third, Stephen Jay Gould's "Our Allotted Lifetimes" (NR 260, SE 148), challenges us to think about death differently. You might assign all three. Thomas' essay, brief and direct, moves between the emotional and medical aspects of dying; Kübler-Ross' looks at dying patients and their needs and rights; Gould's measures our life span against that of other mammals and concludes that we live an exceptionally long time.

Dr. Elisabeth Kübler-Ross, a Swiss psychologist, was a pioneer in examining attitudes toward death and dying; *On Death and Dying,* from which this essay comes, was published in 1969. In it Kübler-Ross announces as her intended audience professionals who work with the dying, like chaplains and social workers (paragraph 2), and her excursus on the communications of the dying may be of particular interest to them. The book, however, was a best-seller that clearly transcended any particular audience she may have had in mind. Kübler-Ross, in the selection reprinted here, moves through various kinds of material—experience, observation, reading, analysis—to make a series of related points about patients and their needs and the often-competing needs of those who take care of them and the families who arrange for their care. Since the publication of *On Death and Dying,* medical technology has made it possible to prolong life almost indefinitely and court cases have complicated what Kübler-Ross regards as patients' rights. Students will probably have some familiarity with these issues and may need to be taken back to the essay itself.

Analytical Considerations

1. You might ask students to reread paragraphs 15 to 17 and consider what Kübler-Ross' vignette, her personal report, enables her to say and to imply. Implication may be of two sorts: the texture and emotional resonance of the episode she recollects and its modern obverse. How would this farmer die today?
2. Consider what Kübler-Ross and Thomas, in "The Long Habit," say about the mechanical prolongation of life.
3. See Kübler-Ross on avoidance techniques (paragraph 22). You might ask students to discuss these and other techniques for avoiding unpleasant truths. What would be the consequences of speaking plainly and acting openly?

Suggested Writing Assignments

1. Write an essay in which you focus on your own experience of the death of someone you love. Frame it by considering Kübler-Ross'

analysis of how the treatment of the dying reflects the needs of the living.

2. Kübler-Ross' attention to death and dying is repeated now in college courses on death and dying. If your institution offers one, get a copy of its syllabus, interview a couple of students who are taking or have taken it, and write an essay in which you describe the course and analyze what you take to be Kübler-Ross' influence on it.

3. Do library research on one court case involving the mechanical prolongation of life. Look in particular at who is on each side and what arguments their lawyers make. Write an essay in which you describe and analyze the arguments of each side with respect to the rights of patients and the needs of others as Kübler-Ross conceives them and as you conceive them.

4. Read sections of Philippe Aries' *The Hour of Our Death* (1981). Giving proper credit to both Aries and Kübler-Ross, describe and analyze a set of customs surrounding death that Aries describes in terms of Kübler-Ross' scheme, that is, the rights of patients and the needs of others.

Additional questions on this essay will be found in the text (NR 258–60, SE 147–48).

STEPHEN JAY GOULD

Our Allotted Lifetimes

The Norton Reader, p. 260; Shorter Edition, p. 148

Two essays in this section discuss the feelings that attend our thinking about death: Lewis Thomas' "The Long Habit" (NR 247, SE 136) and Elisabeth Kübler-Ross' "On the Fear of Death."(NR 252, SE 140). A third, Stephen Jay Gould's "Our Allotted Lifetimes," challenges us to think about death differently. You might assign all three. Thomas' essay, brief and direct, moves between the emotional and medical aspects of dying; Kübler-Ross' looks at dying patients and their needs and rights; Gould's measures our life span against that of other mammals and concludes that we live an exceptionally long time, "longer than a mammal of our body size should."

The above is just one of Stephen Jay Gould's arresting formulations. He is a biologist, an historian of science, and a superb popularizer; this essay, like others, was first published in the column he writes for *Natural History* magazine. You will want to make sure that students understand his explanations of scaling theory and relative (and absolute) time. You may also want to consider with them his presentation of mathematical information in both numbers and words. But it's his larger strategy that deserves most attention: By considering humans under the category mammal, Gould reframes and provokes us to rethink death.

Gould, like Desmond Morris in "Territorial Behavior" (NR 188, SR 94), may be said to draw reductive parallels between humans and mammals, emphasizing similarities and neglecting differences. He neglects our feelings with respect to our own deaths; when he alludes to our feelings, it is with respect to the death of a pet mouse or gerbil, and he writes them off: "our personal grief, of course, is quite another matter; with this, science does not deal" (paragraph 8). Nevertheless, his conclusion that we may "try to bend an ancient world to our purposes" suggests that he accepts the natural order of things, as both Thomas and Kübler-Ross do.

Analytical Considerations

1. Have students, probably in groups, take each others' pulses and measure each others' rates of breathing. Are they in accord with Gould's ratios of four to one? Have them explain the ratios; also have them explain how many heartbeats and breaths they can anticipate in their allotted lifetimes.
2. Have students mark Gould's arresting formulations and look at his use of words, sentence structure, and analogies. You might also have students experiment with rewriting them to diminish their force.
3. Direct students' attention to the long parenthesis in paragraph 7. What problems is Gould trying to avoid with this parenthesis? What problems does he create with it?

Suggested Writing Assignments

1. Locate and read the essay on neoteny that Gould refers to in paragraph 7. Write an essay in which you explain it in reference to "Our Allotted Lifetimes." You might also add a paragraph of conjecture as to why he skirts the subject in "Our Allotted Lifetimes."
2. Construct what you take to be Gould's views on the mechanical prolongation of life. Write an essay in which you compare them with what either Thomas in "The Long Habit" or Kübler-Ross in

"On the Fear of Death" say about it.

3. Read Gould's other essays in *The Norton Reader*: "The Terrifying Normalcy of AIDS" (NR 702, SE 424), "Darwin's Middle Road" (NR 1013, SE 617), and "Scientific Error" (NR 1003, SE 634). Describe some of his strategies in writing about science. Or consider his views on what science includes and what it excludes.

Additional questions on this essay will be found in the text (NR 264–65, SE 153).

EDUCATION

JOHN HOLT

How Teachers Make Children Hate Reading

The Norton Reader, p. 271; Shorter Edition, p. 154

The late John Holt, after ten years as a teacher, wrote *How Children Fail* (1964), a critical analysis of American education, followed by *How Children Learn* (1967). "How Teachers Make Children Hate Reading," which appeared in *Redbook* magazine in 1967, is a compendium of both: how children fail to learn and yet how they succeed in learning that complex of subjects referred to in elementary school as language arts (Holt's editorial comment on that term, in paragraph 33, is *Ugh!*). Holt writes for a general rather than a professional audience: In paragraphs 44 and 45, for example, he addresses parents. He includes a lot of information about what works and what doesn't through vignettes, a few of them about particular students, most of them about particular classes. His essay disperses itself into a set of precepts, how-not-to and how-to. You might ask students to trace Holt's assumptions about learning, children as learners, and the value of reading and writing through these precepts.

Running through Holt's essay is another theme, the education of John Holt, the teacher. Most revealing, probably, is the opening vignette, in which Holt's professional wisdom is challenged by his sister's experiential wisdom. As the essay proceeds, Holt again and again invents new and more successful modes of teaching that run counter to professionally sanctioned modes; only *after* he invents the writing derby, for example, does he find that S. I. Hayakawa has invented nonstop writing (paragraphs 28 and 29). Holt's inventions always succeed. You might ask students to consider his antiprofessional bent. Is it possible to codify his wisdom as professional wisdom? Some twenty-five years after Holt published "How Teachers Make Students Hate Reading," has any of his wisdom become professional wisdom?

Analytical Considerations

1. You might ask students to look at Holt's advice to parents

(paragraphs 44 and 45). What assumptions does he make about parents' circumstances and their involvement with their children's education? Are these assumptions, from your students' experience, legitimate?

2. Ask students about their own education in reading and writing, particularly with respect to how much of Holt's experiential wisdom has become professional wisdom since 1967, when "How Teachers Make Children Hate Reading" was published. The results are hard to predict. In general, since Holt's essay appeared, the teaching of writing has changed more than the teaching of reading, but not uniformly.

3. You might follow up Analytical Consideration 2 with students' responses to Holt's methods of teaching reading and writing. What force does their experience have, individually and collectively?

4. What do your students think about Holt's advice on reading, "Find something, dive into it, take the good parts, skip the bad parts, get what you can out of it, go on to something else" (paragraph 21)?

Suggested Writing Assignments

1. Two antitheses are often used with respect to pedagogy: teaching versus learning, teacher centered versus student centered. Write an essay in which you define these antitheses using Holt's essay and amplifying them with your own experience. Is Holt firmly on one side or the other? Are you?

2. According to Holt, "we make books and reading a constant source of possible failure and public humiliation" (paragraph 13). Write an essay based on your own experience, observation, and reading in which you discuss education as failure and humiliation. Are failure and humiliation chiefly associated with reading?

3. Imagine yourself sending Holt's "How Teachers Make Children Hate Reading" to one of your English teachers. Write a letter to accompany the essay.

4. Locate two or three instances from your own education where your experiential wisdom ran counter to the apparently professional wisdom of your teachers. Use them in an essay in which you evaluate the nature and importance of personal experience in teaching. Would you generalize your own experience, at least of the instances you choose, into professional wisdom?

Additional questions on this essay will be found in the text (NR 280, SE 162–63).

JAMES THURBER

University Days

The Norton Reader, p. 290; Shorter Edition, p. 163

James Thurber is known for his stories, fables, and cartoons. "University Days," published in 1933, is an example of deadpan humor. Thurber creates himself literally and metaphorically as a near-blind innocent who stumbles though the strange world of the university, trying to understand its odd customs without much success. The essay is a series of vignettes: botany lab, economics, gym, journalism, and ROTC. The other undergraduates who figure in it are even dimmer than Thurber. You might, for example, look at Bolenciecwcz's adventure in economics as a stripped-down sequence of cartoons (paragraphs 5 to 12).

"University Days" is a comic essay, not a critique of higher education, and few students will take it as seriously critical. Considering how we know how to take it can be a useful exercise. You might take it as critique yourself and let students argue against your view. They should be able to point to Thurber's exaggerations, his use of idiosyncratic and extreme examples as representative; they may be less likely to point to his verbal wit, to the comic precision of his language.

Analytical Considerations

1. You might look at Thurber's creation of a comic persona, perhaps with reference to his literal and metaphoric blindness. What, in the various vignettes, does Thurber not see?
2. You might look also at comedy in Thurber's fables: "The Rabbits Who Caused All the Trouble" (NR 908, SE 530) and "The Owl Who Was God" (NR 1176). Can students generalize about Thurber's comic techniques?

Suggested Writing Assignments

1. Rewrite Thurber's essay as a serious critique of some elements of higher education. Use his material and add to it; using idiosyncratic and extreme examples as representative makes for comedy, not critique.
2. Find one incident from your university days that will yield to a Thurber-like treatment and write about it.

Additional questions on this essay will be found in the text (NR 295, SE 168–69).

ADRIENNE RICH

Taking Women Students Seriously

The Norton Reader, p. 295; Shorter Edition, p. 169

Adrienne Rich is a poet as well as an essayist. Born in 1929, she graduated from Radcliffe College in 1951, the year her first book of poems was published; her early poetry antedates the women's movement. In "Taking Women Students Seriously," an address given to teachers of women, Rich professes her intention not to lecture but to "create a context, delineate a background" for discussion. She begins with her own education and her experience teaching minority students as well as women students. "The personal is political"—this is a maxim of the women's movement and an enabling principle of consciousness-raising. It is also a strategy of feminist writing; see, for example, Evelyn Fox Keller's "Women in Science: A Social Analysis" (NR 1020, SE 625).

Rich sets in parallel form the questions discussed by instructors of minority students and the questions she came to ask about teaching women. Both minorities and women are disadvantaged, and the pedagogy appropriate to one has parallels with the pedagogy appropriate to the other. Note Rich's emphasis on activity versus passivity, questioning rather than accepting. Her discussion of women as students leads to a discussion of women in society: The academy mirrors society at large in putting women down or not taking them seriously.

Analytical Considerations

1. You might ask students to review the personal elements in Rich's essay and their political meanings. "The personal is political"— political in what sense or senses?
2. In paragraphs 8 and 9, Rich discusses what she calls "the precariously budgeted, much-condescended-to area of women's studies." What does women's studies teach, and why, according to

Rich, do women need to learn these things?

3. Rich speaks of both women and men as if gender unites them more than other circumstances—large circumstances of social and economic class, of race and ethnicity and small circumstances of infinite variety—divide them. She creates universals that may well be false. Consider the following: "Men in general think badly: in disjuncture from their personal lives, claiming objectivity where the most irrational passions seethe" (paragraph 16). Does Rich's generalization suggest a counter-generalization about how women think?

4. "Feminists are depicted in the media," Rich says, "as 'shrill,' 'strident,' 'puritanical,' or 'humorless,' and the lesbian choice—the choice of the woman-identified woman—as pathological or sinister" (paragraph 12). The last became Rich's choice. Does she run the risk of such labels in this essay? Does she care? Who is her audience, and what assumptions does she make about them?

Suggested Writing Assignments

1. From your experience and observation (of high school or college or both), are women students taken seriously? Do faculty members treat them in the same way as male students? Do male students regard them as equals? You might also consider differences between female and male teachers and between fields of study, for example, between education and engineering, or English and physics.

2. Read Fox Keller's "Women in Science: A Social Analysis" and write an essay in which you discuss how Rich and Keller present and link the personal and the political. Are their examples sufficient to warrant their generalizations about sexism in American higher education?

3. Read Rich's "When We Dead Awaken: Writing as Re-Vision" (NR 495), published in *On Lies, Secrets, and Silence: Selected Prose, 1966–1978* (1979), in which she reviews her education while tracing her development as a woman poet and a feminist poet. Write an essay in which you discuss how she presents and links the personal and the political. What, in Rich's view, are the politics of poetry?

4. Read Gloria Steinem's "The Good News Is: These Are Not the Best Years of Your Life" (NR 515, SE 313). On the face of things, Steinem and Rich take opposed views of women's college experience. Write an essay in which you discuss how you think their views are opposed, why you think they are opposed, and the

extent to which you can reconcile them.

5. If you have a women's studies program at your institution, find out more about it. What are its aims, what courses does it teach, and who teaches them? Interview some students, some faculty, and/or both who are active in women's studies. Write an essay in which you discuss women's studies at your institution. Enunciate your own position with respect to women's studies as part of your discussion.

6. Some institutions have undertaken what is called gender balancing the curriculum, that is, introducing women into courses that previously focused on men. If your institution has undertaken gender balancing, find out more about what has been done. What are its aims, what courses have been changed, and how? Interview some students in these courses and/or some faculty who teach them. Write an essay in which you discuss gender balancing at your institution and enunciate your own position on this issue.

WILLIAM ZINSSER

College Pressures

The Norton Reader, p. 310; Shorter Edition, p. 176

William Zinsser, a journalist and writer, taught at Yale University from 1971 to 1979 and served, he explains, as master of Branford College. "College Pressures" was published in 1979; students will probably notice that room, board, and tuition in most private colleges then cost *as much as* $7,000 and that students might leave college with debts of *as much as* $5,000. (What are room, board, and tuition now?) Zinsser introduces "College Pressures" with notes from students and then, in an odd maneuver, first generalizes and then limits their relevance: "students like the ones who wrote those notes can also be found on campuses from coast to coast—especially in New England and at many other private colleges across the country that have high academic standards and highly motivated students." You might ask students if Zinsser's claim is too large or too small? Is it out of place? Is it out of date? Are most/many/some/ students still harried, driven by external and internal pressures, and career oriented? Which students, and where are they to be found?

"College Pressures" appeared in a little-known magazine, *Blair &*

Ketchum's Country Journal. Who does Zinsser think his audience is? What evidence is there in the essay? Is it written to students, to professors, to parents, to outsiders? Or what elements of it seem directed to each of these groups?

Zinsser uses a four-part classificatory scheme in characterizing the pressures on students as economic, parental, peer, and self-induced. His scheme does not provide structure to his entire essay, however; it is elaborately framed, and the divisions according to kinds of pressure are not only weighted with illustrations but also cross-referenced (see, for example, paragraphs 15 through 19 and 24). Zinsser apparently sees his classificatory scheme as rhetorically useful in ordering his material but distorting in compartmentalizing it. You might want to discuss the values of using classification *within* an essay rather than as the framework for the entire essay.

Analytical Considerations

1. Zinsser combines personal experience with description, analysis, and explicit and implied prescription. You might have students locate personal passages and discuss their contribution to the essay. What is Zinsser's authority to describe, analyze, and advise, and how does he claim it in this essay?
2. You might also ask students to imagine Zinsser's four-part classificatory scheme as organizing his entire essay. What parts of "College Pressures" would remain, what parts would go? What would be the effect of these omissions?
3. "Where's the payoff on the humanities?" Zinsser inquires (paragraph 20). Ask students to define the payoff Zinsser illustrates. You might also have them look at other payoffs, such as those Wayne C. Booth offers in "Is There Any Knowledge That a Man *Must* Have?" (NR 337, SE 195).

Suggested Writing Assignments

1. What are the pressures on college students today? Write an essay in which you describe and analyze then, perhaps using evidence from Zinsser to suggest that some pressures remain the same.
2. "Where's the payoff on the humanities?" Zinsser asks. Write your own answer to this question, drawing on your personal experience and that of your peers.

Additional questions on this essay will be found in the text (NR 317, SE 183–84).

WILLIAM G. PERRY, JR.

Examsmanship and the Liberal Arts: A Study in Educational Epistemology

The Norton Reader, p. 318; Shorter Edition, p. 184

William G. Perry, Jr.'s urbane and erudite discussion of examsmanship, while it contains much of interest to students, is not addressed *to* or written *for* students; it was published in *Examining in Harvard College: A Collection of Essays* (1964), a volume written by members of the Harvard faculty and probably addressed to them as well. Perry approaches "educational epistemology" (you might ask students, after they have read the essay, to define it) through a story that, were it told simply, is comic: "the picture of a bright student attempting to outwit his professor while his professor takes pride in not being outwitted," Perry observes, "is certainly ridiculous" (paragraph 4). Perry's elaborate irony and extended explanations defuse its comedy. What students will understand is the surprising use to which Perry puts the story of Metzger's prank: he not only defends it as harmless but also, and more importantly, defends the section man's grade of A as just. You might want to look at Perry's narrative strategies as preparation for this reversal: a less complicated telling might turn the story into a trickster tale.

Perry's educational epistemology involves framing, in which a fact becomes "an observation or operation performed in a frame of reference" (paragraph 40). You might, with this observation in mind, direct students back to Perry's account of Metzger's examination: he wrote about framing because he had no facts to frame. In addition, you should probably ask students to discriminate between this educational epistemology and their own cruder one, which Perry describes as finding "the right mean" between particulars and generalizations. They are not the same: "The problem is not quantitative," Perry writes, "nor does its solution lie on a continuum between the particular and the general" (paragraph 25).

Perry calls framing "bull," facts "cow." The first comes from "bull session": shooting the breeze, talking loudly and authoritatively. "Cow" is Perry's invented opposite, and the genders of the pair are unfortunate, inasmuch as thought becomes male, data reporting female. Perry, again surprisingly, defends "bull," redeeming it in an academic context from its pejorative sense. While framed facts are best, if it comes to choosing between them, framing is better—even though students who present unframed facts on examinations are seldom given grades as low as they deserve. Perry also analyzes the mistaken educational epistemology of elementary and high schools: students are given high grades for remembering facts and graded down for misremembering them.

Analytical Considerations

1. Perry has divided his essay into four parts: an introduction followed by three numbered sections. These divisions suggest distinct sections related one to the other. Identify the focus of each section and its relation to what precedes and what follows.
2. What does Perry mean by "bull" and "cow"? How does he oppose them to each other? You might ask students first to locate Perry's definitions of "bull" and "cow" and then write their own. Is it necessary to provide examples to define terms? This exercise might profitably done in groups.
3. How necessary are Perry's terms "bull" and "cow"? Can students find gender-neutral terms to fit Perry's and their definitions? See Analytic Consideration 1., above.
4. Ask students to look at paragraph 24, the "productive wedding" of "bull" and "cow." How do Perry's gendered terms proliferate into metaphors? What are the consequences?
5. Perry, confronting the moral issues that "bull" raises, asserts: "Too early a moral judgment is precisely what stands between many able students and a liberal education" (paragraph 5); education of the right sort leads "not away from, but *through* the arts of gamesmanship to a new trust" (paragraph 40). Ask students to discuss these assertions with reference to the essay as a whole.
6. See Perry's account of the history examination that entering students at Harvard and Radcliffe are asked to grade (paragraphs 48–49). How do the results warrant his generalization that "better students in the better high schools and preparatory schools are being allowed to inquire"? Is this a qualified generalization or a snobbish one?

Suggested Writing Assignments

1. Write an essay addressed to college freshmen in which you pass on what is important in Perry's essay. You may of course include what Perry says as advice about getting good grades. But grades, Perry observes, reflect an educational epistemology. Do not slight epistemological issues.
2. Write an essay in which you describe and analyze the educational

epistemology underlying your high school education. Introduce the essay with a fully developed incident.
3. Perry suggests that educational epistemologies differ according to field of study, with English teachers privileging "bull" and science teachers "cow" (paragraph 38). Is this true of your experience? Write an essay in which you contrast your experience of "bullish" and "cowish" fields of study.
4. Read Wayne C. Booth's "Is There Any Knowledge That a Man *Must* Have?" (NR 337, SE 195). Write an essay in which you compare Booth's educational epistemology with Perry's as it appears in "Examsmanship and the Liberal Arts: A Study in Educational Epistemology." You may find it helpful to consider, as categories, the liberal arts, modes of thinking, and what is thought about. What does each emphasize? Are their differences differences of emphasis or of content?

Additional questions on this essay will be found in the text (NR 328 , SE 195).

WAYNE C. BOOTH

Is There Any Knowledge That a Man *Must* Have?

The Norton Reader, p. 337; Shorter Edition, p 195

"Is There Any Knowledge That a Man *Must* Have?" began as an address to undergraduates at a conference at the University of Chicago: Wayne C. Booth, then a professor of English (and now professor emeritus) observes, "I look at you out there, knowing that some of you are physics majors" (paragraph 27). The year was 1967. The essay has a clearly delineated structure. Nevertheless, connections among its divisions are often implied rather than explained, and they are rather loose. Students will probably have to be pushed to make them; you and they may decide that they are too loose. About half of the essay (paragraphs 6–31) surveys four possible definitions of "the creature we would educate." Three, which Booth denies, are metaphoric: a machine, an animal, an ant citizen of an anthill. The fourth, which he accepts, is literal: a creature "resistant to our efforts at metaphor or analogy or image-making" (paragraph 29) and consequently unique.

The remaining half of the essay (paragraphs 32–48) concerns education. The education Booth advocates he calls "liberal"—and it may be useful to remind students that the root of *liberal* is the Latin *liber*, or free. The knowledge he advocates is "the knowledge or capacity or power to act freely as a man" (paragraph 33). Again Booth postpones explanation, turning to models for acquiring knowledge before he turns to knowledge itself. When he does, he identifies three what he calls *domains*: nature and Nature, art, and practical wisdom. Then—and only then—does he offer a definition of acting freely: thinking one's own thoughts, experiencing beauty for oneself, and choosing one's own actions (paragraph 47).

Booth actually wrote that "a man" can be human "*if* he has learned to think his own thoughts, experience beauty for himself, and choose his own actions"; what is the effect of the paraphrase "thinking one's own thoughts, experiencing beauty for oneself, and choosing one's own actions" (above)? When Booth wrote "Is There Any Knowledge that a Man *Must* Have," the use of "man" as a generic was not often questioned; today it is questioned, strenuously, and the essay as he wrote it sounds assertively masculinist. Booth himself would no longer use "man" as a generic; see the note appended to his essay. Moreover, while he sees false generics as contributing to women's educational disempowerment, he looks beyond them to larger issues of educating women in a male-dominated society.

Analytical Considerations

1. How do the metaphoric definitions that Booth denies—a machine, an animal, an ant citizen of an anthill—stand in relation to the literal definition that he accepts?
2. What models for acquiring knowledge does Booth accept?
3. With Booth's definition of freedom in mind, you might ask students to return again to the education of machines, animals, and ant citizens of an anthill. How does each form of education deny freedom as Booth understands it?
4. Booth's three domains of knowledge do not align themselves with the general education and/or distribution requirements of most colleges and universities, nor does Booth intend them too; see his comments in paragraph 47.
5. You might ask students, perhaps in groups, to consider specific courses they are taking and the domains they encompass. Booth appears to slight natural science—but does he?
6. Does Booth's use of "man" as a generic sound assertively

masculinist to students? You might refer them to "Man, Its Compounds, and Other False Generics" (G 000) for substitutions. Have them make some and then discuss them, perhaps in groups.

Suggested Writing Assignments

1. Read carefully a general statement of educational aims in your college catalog and write an essay in which you construct the metaphor or metaphors for the "creature to be educated" it implies.
2. Read William G. Perry, Jr., "Examsmanship and the Liberal Arts: A Study in Educational Epistemology" (NR 318, SE 184). Write an essay in which you compare Perry's educational epistemology with Booth's as it appears in "Is There Any Knowledge That a Man *Must* Have?" You may find it helpful to consider, as categories, the liberal arts, modes of thinking, and what is thought about. What does each emphasize? Are their differences differences of emphasis or of content?
3. Read Booth's "Is There Any Knowledge that a Woman Must Have?" in *The Vocation of a Teacher* (1988). Compare the points Booth makes in this essay with the points Adrienne Rich makes in "Taking Women Students Seriously" (NR 295, SE 169). Write an essay in which you discuss whether Rich would approve of Booth as a teacher of women, and whether you would. What about Booth as a teacher of men? Are the two antithetical? Be sure to make clear your own involvement with these issues.

WILLIAM J. BENNETT

Address

The Norton Reader, p. 353; Shorter Edition, p. 211

This essay is an address delivered in 1986, when William J. Bennett was still Secretary for Education (during Reagan's presidency), on the occasion of Harvard's 350th birthday celebration. Bennett explains the circumstances and celebrates (at least) some of his experiences at Harvard before turning to criticize American education, particularly higher education; as he owns in paragraph 8, he had already established himself as a critic. Students, Bennett says, deserve from colleges and universities "real and sustained attention to their intellectual and their moral well-being" (paragraph 11).

Bennett firmly specifies what is required for students' intellectual well-being: "at a minimum, a systematic familiarity with our own, Western tradition of learning: with the classical and Jewish-Christian heritage, the facts of American and European history, the political organization of western societies, the great works of Western art and literature, the major achievements of the scientific disciplines" (paragraph 11). These, according to Bennett, constitute a "liberal education." You might ask students to read "Is There Any Knowledge That a Man *Must* Have?" (NR 337, SE 195) and notice how, for all that Booth's title suggests content, he focuses on modes of thinking, Bennett on content.

Bennett is less specific about students' moral well-being and how higher education is to inculcate it. He is, however, quick to point out that college faculty, ready to improve the world at large, are reluctant to attend to the improvement of their charges at home. He advocates for all students the personal attention he gave the freshmen he advised at Harvard and thinks that faculty and students irresponsibly give students too much freedom. Institutions and students vary: not all colleges are impersonal, not all students want them to stand in *loco parentis*. How much personal attention do students get at your institution? How much do they want? And how did personal attention figure in their decision to attend (and their parents' decision to send them)?

The debates over multiculturalism and political correctness (or PC) prefigured in Bennett's address have become more acrimonious since. The liberal education he prescribes is western and Eurocentric, though he may be said to gesture toward nonwestern traditions with his remark that students, lacking knowledge of their own, "have no standpoint from which to appreciate any other tradition, or even to *have* a sense of tradition" (paragraph 12). He deplores what will come to be known as Political Correctness, for the ideas he finds colleges and universities hostile to are conservative ones.

Analytic Considerations

1. You might ask students to look at the general education or distribution requirements of your institution and the explanation that accompanies them. Does your institution prescribe what Bennett considers a liberal education? Is it sequential and purposive or hit-and-miss—Bennett's metaphors are the "smorgasbord" and the "Chinese menu" (paragraph 12)?
2. Bennett describes the response to his criticism metaphorically:

faculty and administrators look at the university as if it were a religious institution (paragraph 8). He returns to this metaphor in paragraphs 21–22. You might ask students to reread these paragraphs and consider how Bennett uses metaphor not only to describe the university but also to criticize it.

3. Money figures largely in Bennett's criticism. As Secretary of Education, his criticism seemed like a threat: federal money might be withdrawn if colleges and universities did not respond to it. You might point out to students the extent to which federal (and state) money supports their education and discuss the consequences of Bennett's position. Does he who pays the piper call the tune? What do they think ought to be the relations between education and the state?

Suggested Writing Assignments

1. Imagine yourself going back somewhere—to high school, to college, to some sort of institution with which you have been affiliated—on a public occasion to deliver an address. You decide to offer a critical view derived from your own experience. How do you criticize without seeming like a spoilsport, and how do you use your own experience without making your criticism sound like a private grievance? Write your address.

2. Read Wayne C. Booth's "Is There Any Knowledge That a Man *Must* Have?" (NR 337, SE 195) with particular attention to Booth's analysis of "the creature to be educated." Describe and analyze Bennett's "creature to be educated." You may use Booth's definitions or ignore them.

3. The academics Bennett quotes to support his argument that colleges and universities are intolerant of conservative ideas (and conservatives) are James Billington and James Q. Wilson. Do library research on them, their ideas, and their careers and write an essay in which you comment on how and why Bennett uses them.

4. Read Bennett's *To Reclaim a Legacy: A Report on the Humanities in Higher Education* (1984) and write an essay in which you analyze his account of the humanities' relationship to what, in this address, he calls "moral discernment" (paragraph 19).

LANGUAGE AND COMMUNICATION

RICHARD MITCHELL

The Voice of Sisera

The Norton Reader, p. 373; Shorter Edition, p. 221

Language is more than a form of communication; it is also, as Richard Mitchell argues, a means of social and political control. Mitchell illustrates this thesis by drawing on a historical range of examples: the story of Jael, the Kenite woman who slew the warrior Sisera (probably, according to Mitchell, because he spoke the language of a conqueror rather than Jael's native dialect); the Norman conquest of England in 1066 and the imposition of French as the official language; the use of French by the Russian aristocracy among itself, with Russian reserved for "servants, very small children, and domestic animals"; and so on down through the "officialese" of American income tax forms, law courts, and other kinds of bureaucracy. Mitchell ends his essay with a plea for universal education as a means of combating the snobbish, even dangerous, tendency of language to exert social control. You might want to ask your students whether or not education can, in fact, combat this tendency and what kind of education might be effective in doing so.

Analytical Considerations

1. Ask students to look up the story of Jael and Sisera in the Bible, Judges iv and v. How does Mitchell reinterpret the story? What explanation does the Bible give of Jael's motive for murder? What motive does Mitchell suggest?
2. What does Mitchell mean by "the voice of Sisera"? Note the places in the essay in which this phrase recurs. How does it function as a refrain?
3. What is the structure of Mitchell's essay? Students might note that it presents the problem of language as social control, followed by a possible solution. Or they might note that Mitchell presents his historical examples first, followed by examples from our everyday lives. Or they might note (as in Analytical Consideration 2) that the phrase "voice of Sisera" functions as a refrain to tie disparate

examples together. You might use this discussion to suggest that essays can achieve "structure" using more than one strategy.

4. Early in the essay, Mitchell refers to the Norman conquest of England and the imposition of French on an Anglo-Saxon population. Only late in the essay does Mitchell illustrate the effects on modern English—in his distinction between *forgive* and *pardon*. Ask students to look up the etymology of these two words or, more generally, to leaf through a dictionary to determine which words tend to come from Anglo-Saxon, French, Latin, or Greek origins. For what reasons might a writer choose a word from one (versus another) of these sources?

Suggested Writing Assignments

1. Analyze the language of an official letter you have received, whether from the government, your college or university, or some commercial institution. Is it "Siserean" language? If so, what is its intended effect? If not, what other effect is intended?

2. Find a piece of "Siserean" language, and rewrite it so that the effect is not one of a ruler communicating to the ruled. What might be the function of your revised piece of communication? Is it as effective as the original?

3. Narrate a personal experience in which someone used "the voice of Siscra" to control your behavior. As you narrate, convey both a clear sense of the actual language used and your response to it.

Additional questions on this essay will be found in the text (NR 378, SE 226–27).

GLORIA NAYLOR

"Mommy, What Does 'Nigger' Mean?"

The Norton Reader, pp. 378; Shorter Edition, p. 227

A graduate of Brooklyn College and Yale University, now a contemporary novelist, Gloria Naylor takes up the question of racially loaded language in this essay reprinted from the "Hers" column of the *New York Times*. For Naylor the term *nigger* can, when used by whites, be an insulting, destructive epithet; yet, when used within black communities, it can become a term of endearment, even pride.

By analyzing the examples Naylor gives from her childhood, you might help students to draw out the principles by which Naylor makes this distinction and the position against which Naylor is arguing.

If it seems relevant, you may want to discuss the problem of racially biased language on campuses today. Many colleges and universities have adopted—or are considering adopting—a "code" that would prohibit insulting language based on race, class, gender, or ethnicity. If your campus has such a code, you might analyze it to determine whether it agrees with the principles underlying Naylor's argument or whether it takes the oppositional position to which Naylor alludes in the penultimate paragraph. If your campus has faced any alleged violations of the code, or if students can cite incidents that might violate such a code, ask them to imagine what Naylor's analysis of the incident(s) might be.

Analytical Considerations

1. Like other pieces written for the "Hers" column, Naylor's essay uses a combination of personal experience and impersonal generalization. Why does Naylor choose to begin with two paragraphs of generalization rather than with her third-grade experience?
2. What makes Naylor's narrative of her third-grade experience so powerful? Help students analyze the concise, objective style, the effect of words like *nymphomaniac* and *necrophiliac;* and the unstated assumptions about black students that Naylor writes against.
3. The bulk of Naylor's essay recounts memories in which nigger occurs in nonderogatory contexts. What are the possible connotations of the term as used by blacks? Why does Naylor wish to show the richness of this term within the black community? How does this richness contrast with the starkness of the white third grader's language?
4. In the penultimate paragraph, Naylor summarizes a position against which she is arguing: "that the use of the word nigger at this social stratum of the black community [is] an internalization of racism." Ask students what evidence they might bring to support the opposing argument—and why Naylor treats it only briefly when and where she does.
5. Naylor never tells us how her mother answered the question, "What does 'nigger' mean?" Instead, she simply concludes, "And since she [her mother] knew that I had to grow up in America, she took

me in her lap and explained." Why does Naylor end this way?

6. What persona does Naylor create in this essay—and how? What kind of person do we imagine her to be? Why is this persona important to her argument?

Suggested Writing Assignments

1. Write an essay about the use of the term *nigger* in which you disagree with Naylor and take the opposing position that she alludes to in the penultimate paragraph: "that the use of the word nigger at this social stratum of the black community [is] an internalization of racism."

2. If you come from a racial or ethnic minority, write an analysis of a term that can have negative or positive meaning, depending on the context in which it is used.

3. Has the use of the word *nigger* changed within the black community since Naylor's childhood? If you come from that community, write an essay analyzing your own memories of how the term was (and still is) used. Alternatively, interview black students on your campus about the uses of the term and their responses.

4. Write an essay about your own experiences with a word that someone used to insult or denigrate. As you analyze your experience, try to draw out the various connotations of the word, as Naylor does.

MAXINE HONG KINGSTON

Tongue-Tied

The Norton Reader, p. 381; Shorter Edition, p. 230

Maxine Hong Kingston's *The Woman Warrior* combines autobiography with family history, cultural myth, and fictional tale to capture the meaning of growing up female and Chinese-American. As in other sections of her autobiography, Kingston here retells a story originally told by her mother to probe the problem of silence and speech. Although painful, even cruel as Kingston retells it, the story prepares for the complexity of Kingston's linguistic responses, a paradoxical combination of refusing speech and speaking out, depending on the context.

If you have read Richard Mitchell's "The Voice of Sisera" (NR

221, SE 373), you might ask students whether his theory of language as a form of political dominance and social control applies to Kingston's situation: Why can't she speak in English school, for example, when she can speak, shout, even scream in Chinese school? If you have read Richard Rodriguez's "Aria" (NR 385, SE 234,) you might compare the essays to explore the complex patterns of gender, ethnicity, and class that effect a student's ability to speak. Such a discussion will prevent students from assuming that only one factor creates a condition of silence. Both Kingston and Rodriguez, female and male, suffer from an inability to speak in school; yet Kingston can speak at home and in Chinese school, whereas Rodriguez notes the growing silences at the family dinner table. Furthermore, learning a new language affects family members in different ways: the mothers in these two families learn to speak out in English, whereas Rodriguez's father (Kingston does not mentions hers) becomes quiet, almost shy as his family learns its second language.

Analytical Considerations

1. Encourage students to interpret the story that Kingston's mother tells. What meanings do they see? What meanings does Kingston emphasize?
2. How does Kingston convey the differences between being a person, an "I," in English versus being one in Chinese? What other strategies does she use to explain the differences between Chinese and Americans?
3. Compare Kingston's experiences in grade school with Rodriguez's as described in "Aria." How and why are they similar or different?

Suggested Writing Assignments

1. If you had difficulty speaking in school, write an essay in which you describe and analyze your experience. Did you face obstacles similar to or different from those Kingston describes?
2. Retell a story that your mother, father, or grandparent told to communicate appropriate (or inappropriate) behavior within your ethnic community. Try to capture the richness of the story, as well as your responses to it.
3. Is silence always a mark of social control? Can it also be a form of resistance? Analyze Kingston's or Rodriguez's account to suggest ways in which the author is being both controlled and resisting control.

RICHARD RODRIGUEZ

Aria

The Norton Reader, p. 385; Shorter Edition, p. 234

"Aria" is the first chapter of the autobiography *Hunger of Memory: The Education of Richard Rodriguez* (1982). This selection comes from the end of that chapter, in which Rodriguez draws on the memories he has narrated and makes his case most explicitly—and forcefully—against modern bilingual education. When *Hunger of Memory* was first published, it provoked heated controversy among Spanish-speaking Americans. Rodriguez opposes modern bilingual education not only because he believes that it delays the acquisition of English so crucial to American citizenship but, more important, because he believes that all education requires the assumption of a "public" voice and the loss of "private" language. To avoid the process of loss *and* gain is, for Rodriguez, to undermine or sentimentalize education.

If you have students whose first, "public" language is not English, this essay provides an occasion for allowing them to speak for—or against—the arguments of a professional writer. If they agree with Rodriguez, you might ask them to narrate incidents that support his views and the analysis he provides. If they disagree, you might help them find alternate modes of analysis or counterarguments to define their own positions. Even with classes of students whose only language is English, the issue of the "private" language of home versus the "public" language required at school can provoke an excellent discussion of the process of education.

Analytical Considerations

1. What is Rodriguez's thesis? How does he use the arguments of opponents to define and support his own view? After the opening paragraphs, at what other points does Rodriguez introduce the arguments of his opponents in order to refute them?
2. How does this essay incorporate personal narrative within an argumentative structure? To get at this question, you might analyze the opening sentences of paragraphs 1 through 4, in which Rodriguez articulates his position on bilingual education, versus the

opening sentences of paragraphs 5 through 11, in which Rodriguez condenses his educational experiences into a brief history.

3. Rodriguez's account shows both Spanish and English to be "rich" languages. How—and why—does Rodriguez accomplish this?

4. Rodriguez's autobiographical account of his education might be subtitled "Loss and Gain." What are the gains Rodriguez discusses? the losses? Are there some losses or gains that Rodriguez might be avoiding? Why?

5. What persona does Rodriguez create in this essay—that is, what kind of person do we as readers imagine him to be? Is his persona (in classical rhetoric, the issue of *ethos*) necessary to his argument (the issue of *logos*)?

Suggested Writing Assignments

1. Is the transition from the private language of the home to the public language of the school a necessary part of education? Write an essay, based on your own experience, in which you address this issue.

2. If your first language is something other than English, recount your own experience(s) of learning English in school, either implicitly or explicitly agreeing or disagreeing with Rodriguez's position on bilingual education.

3. Should bilingual education in America be continued or abandoned? Search out other essays on this topic, including some that disagree with Rodriguez's view, and write an essay arguing your own view.

Additional questions on this essay will be found in the text (NR 391–92, SE 240–41).

CASEY MILLER AND KATE SWIFT

Who's in Charge of the English Language?

The Norton Reader, p. 363; Shorter Edition, p. 241

This essay, excerpted from an address given at the annual meeting of the Association of American University Presses (June 26, 1990), argues for gender-neutral language. The argument has been made before, but Miller and Swift provide a tightly organized, well-illustrated version of the doctrine of gender significance in (the

English) language and the need for conscious change. Because their audience is academic, Miller and Swift choose their examples from academic sources (the dictionary, literary criticism, philosophy, history); you might point out this relation between audience and example to your students—and see if they can contribute examples from other contexts.

Most students will have encountered the issue of gender bias in language—and perhaps even rules for avoiding such bias in their writing. You might ask them what they would do, for example, in writing about "a student," whether they would designate that noun with a "he" or "she" and what the implications of their choices might be. (If your college or department has an official statement on gender-neutral language, you might discuss it in conjunction with Miller and Swift's essay, perhaps pointing out the links between the academic "research" in the essay and the practical "application" in a policy statement.) Alternatively, in preparation for reading and discussion, you might ask students about the connotations they bring to the following sets of terms: male-female, masculine-feminine, manly-womanly (the pair used by Miller and Swift).

Analytical Considerations

1. Why do Miller and Swift begin with an illustration from the Book of Genesis about Adam's naming of the animals? Why do they follow up, in the next section, with an analysis of the definitions of *manly* and *womanly* in the most recent *Webster's Third New International Dictionary*?
2. The analysis of *manly* and *womanly* provides a good model for close reading. You might point out the structure—thesis statement, followed by evidence, followed by detailed analysis—and ask students to do similar close reading of another set of gendered terms (those listed above or others from the essay such as hero-heroine, actor-actress).
3. What is the structure of the essay? How do each of the three sections—"Female-Negative-Trivial," "The Slippery Slope," and "Resistance to Change"—advance the argument?
4. From what sources do Miller and Swift draw their evidence? You might ask students to make a list, then perhaps compare it with the sources of evidence that Mairs (NR 392, SE 247) and Naylor (NR 378, SE 227) use in their essays from the "Hers" column of the *New York Times*. How do writers' audiences shape (or even demand) certain kinds of evidence versus others?

5. In their conclusion, Miller and Swift quote George Orwell's "Politics and the English Language" (NR 417, SE 264), included in this section. Ask students to analyze Orwell's essay in terms of Miller and Swift's criteria for gender-neutral language.

Suggested Writing Assignments

1. Analyze an essay from *The Norton Reader* that you think might be guilty of gender-biased language (e.g., Wayne Booth's "Is There Any Knowledge That a Man *Must* Have?" [NR 337, SE 195] or Willard Gaylin, "What You See Is the Real You," [NR 675, SE 414]). What effect does the writer's choice of words have on the meaning the reader takes from the essay?
2. In the section "Female-Negative-Trivial," Miller and Swift use *manly* and *womanly* as their example of terms revealing gender bias. Choose another set of gendered terms, look them up in a modern dictionary, and do a close reading of their connotations.
3. For the next week or two, listen to the language of teachers and students in your classes. Do you hear examples of gender bias? Or do you think that speech in the modern classroom is free from such dichotomies?
4. Using the MLA guidelines reprinted as "'Generic'*He*," rewrite all or part of an essay you consider gender biased (perhaps one you identified for Suggested Writing 1). What stylistic or rhetorical problems did you face in rewriting?

"Generic" *He*

Here and elsewhere in these guidelines, we recommend shifting or recasting passages to avoid discriminatory overtones while preserving the meaning. Although writers who attempt to follow this advice may initially find themselves revising language that appears to convey a sexist message, practice in taking care can lead to a better solution— one in which it will have become natural to select among nonsexist alternatives without having considered the formerly prevalent sexist expression.

The following list summarizes the possibilities and pitfalls to consider in editing out the pseudogeneric masculine pronoun:

1. Recast the sentence in the plural, using *they*, **but avoid** *they* **with singular antecedents.**

2. Shift the person of the pronoun to the first person (*I* or *we*) or the second person (*you*).
3. Use *he* or *she*, or *she* or *he*, if no smoother alternative suggest itself; but avoid repeatedly using such combinations in a passage.
4. Alternate feminine and masculine pronouns in appropriate contexts.
5. Avoid alternative-gender forms requiring slashes and parentheses.
6. Use generic *she* in special circumstances.
7. Edit out the personal pronoun.
8. Use *One*.
9. Preserve the meaning of the original.
10. Preserve the flavor of the original.
11. Avoid introducing stylistic flaws.
12. Avoid needless correction of appropriately used sex-specific pronouns.
13. Avoid incongruity and inconsistent correction.
14. Avoid ambiguity; clarify the terms of analysis.

Man, Its Compounds, and Other False Generics

1. **Do not use *man* "generically."** *Man* no longer functions generically for many people, and instances of ambiguous usage are too common to justify a continued effort to have it refer to either sex. The term *man* should be defined exclusively as an adult male or human being.
2. **Signal that you are not using *man* generically.** Because of the long-standing confusion between "generic" *man* and male *man*, it is, for the present, helpful to let readers know how you are using the term. We repeat Posner's recommendations for signaling sex-specific usage, cited more fully above: (1) use the terms *male* and *female* frequently, even if not deemed relevant in a given instance; (2) if *man* or *men* is used in the sex-specific sense, use *women* early on; and (3) use only pronouns that indicate sex correctly.
3. **Whenever possible, use true generics in place of *man*.** Numerous alternatives to *mankind* are available, including *humankind, human beings, women and men, people, humanity,* and, where appropriate, more specific designations such as our *ancestors, eighteenth-*

century society, Homo sapiens, the human animal, farmers, and *rural populations.*

4. **If you choose to use a male generic, signal your awareness of its problematic status.** In the following passage the author contrasts women's verbal proficiency in most areas of language with their general failure to master "the arcane dialect of the masculine ruling class" The "vast mass" of women's writing, she argues, most of it in the form of letters, diaries, and other occasional writing, "was not set down in the hope of immortality." She continues:

> *Most of it does not assume the posture of the writer addressing (his) public but remains the unaffected discourse between self and self or self and a familiar friend. (Tulsa Studies in Women's Literature 1982)*

The parentheses prevent an automatic identification of the word "writer" with maleness, at the same time emphasizing the most writers who self-consciously wrote for the public were male.

5. **Avoid expressions you dislike.** "I prefer not to use 'humankind,'" wrote an author to the MLA editorial staff during the copyediting of an article for *PMLA*. "I never use it and find it a clumsy word. Surely, 'mankind' need not be abolished from the face of the earth. It's generally in use throughout the Middle Ages and Renaissance." No doubt some other alternative could have been found, however-say, *humanity, human beings, we,* or *people.* For common, but widely disputed terms, it may be helpful to spend some time identifying alternatives you find acceptable. On occasion, of course, an author and an editor may be unable to negotiate perfect agreement; but such is life, and an impasse does not invalidate the effort.

6. **Try to respect others' preferences.** When members of a group specify how they wish to be designated, take their arguments seriously and, if possible, respect their preferences. If a particular usage irritates you, try to find a reasonable alternative. Many writers are more comfortable with *chair*, for example, than with either *chairman* or *chairperson*.

Feminist Alternatives and Related Innovations

1. **Routinely adopt conventional nonsexist alternatives to terms found objectionable.** Considerable effort has been expended, for

example, on identifying or creating rational, plausible gender-neutral job titles. Abandoning *waitress* is no excuse at this point for rejecting nondiscriminatory titles that already exist in the standard vocabulary.

2. **View the more radical feminist lexicon as a resource and draw on it according to your needs.** It would be inappropriate for us to make specific suggestions for using innovations designed, in part, to challenge existing practices. The decision to adopt or forgo them should depend on the nature and purpose of the project: Are traditional terms suitable? Is there value in calling attention to terminology? Are the coinages theoretically necessary or justifiable? How much effort will be required to use them?

3. **Explain or justify your use of any nonstandard alternatives.** Many feminist innovations—structural inventions, idiosyncratic spellings, and neologisms—have by now acquired distinct meanings and connotations that figure significantly in ongoing debates. Thus they are often central to an author's argument. But if the terms have originated outside mainstream English-language writing—in European discourse, in feminist journals, or wherever—an author may encounter an editor unfamiliar with them and may have to demonstrate their theoretical importance. Readers, too may need some background information on a particular usage.

4. **Try to understand and respect the objections of groups to the ways in which they are conventionally labeled.** Seek out intelligent and sensitive alternatives that both you and they can accept. The term *persons with disabilities,* for example, avoids the euphemistic quality of *persons who are physically challenged* as well as the problem raised by totalizing terms like *the disabled,* which identify individuals exclusively by their physical disadvantages.

Gender Marking and Related Usage

1. **In general, avoid feminine suffixes.**
2. **If objectionable feminine suffixes are necessary to refer accurately to another's usage, put them in quotation marks or find another way of showing your disapproval.**
3. **Avoid gender-marked clichés and stereotypes in your writing as you would avoid other kinds of clichés and stereotypes.**
4. **Use names and titles symmetrically.**
   a. Avoid asymmetrical usage: *Miss Austen* versus *Dickens*; *Ms.*

Jane Smith versus *Doctor John Smith*, when both persons hold doctorates.

b. Avoid diminutive or nonprofessional designations of authors: *Jane* (for Jane Austen); *Virginia* or *Mrs. Woolf* (for Virginia Woolf); *Dorothy* or *Dottie* (for Dorothy L. Sayers).

c. Avoid referring to persons by names or titles that they would reject: *Miss Steinem* and *Mrs. Radway* (for the feminists Gloria Steinem and Janice Radway).

d. Similarly, avoid Euro-American or feminist-centered usage when inappropriate; *Ms.Washington* for *Mrs. Booker T. Washington.*

e. Use nonsexist titles with conviction; do not add a superfluous *Miss* or *Mrs.* parenthetically.

f. Avoid the unthinking and exclusive use of male names as touchstones and symbols.

5. Review language for gender stereotypes. In the following example, Cordelia is compared to two figures, one female, the other male. The emphasis is appropriately on their roles, not on their sex.

That she dies as a sacrifice to her sense of filial love and duty puts her into the mythic role of Antigone or even Christ. (PMLA 1983)

6. When using "female" metaphors, avoid stereotyped references to nurturance, passivity, and reproductive functions that are not directly relevant to the text.

NANCY MAIRS

Who Are You?

The Norton Reader, p. 392; Shorter Edition, p. 247

"Who Are You" appeared in the "Hers" column of the *New York Times* (August 13, 1987), as did three other essays in *The Norton Reader*: Joyce Maynard's "Four Generations" (April 12, 1979) (NR 38, SE 26), Gloria Naylor's "Mommy, What Does 'Nigger' Mean?" (February 20, 1986) (NR 378, SE 227), and Letty Cottin Pogrebin's "It Still Takes a Bride and Groom" (July 2, 1989) (NR 532). Because the length of essays in the "Hers" column is limited (approximately 1,000 words), writers must make their points succinctly and choose their examples with precision. In discussing this essay, you might want to concentrate on how Mairs establishes her topic and thesis in her "lead" (the opening two paragraphs), why Mairs limits herself to three main points, and how she chooses and shapes her illustrations.

Like other essays in the "Hers" column, "Who Are You?" provides an example of argumentative writing that incorporates personal experience, of "public" writing that uses a personal voice. If your students tend to separate "personal" writing with an "I" from "impersonal" writing with a thesis, Mairs' essay offers an opportunity to break down this too-simple dichotomy. Mairs is a professional writer who grounds an essay about language practice in personal experience and uses personal experience to arrive at "impersonal" (or general) formulations.

Analytical Considerations

1. Why does Mairs begin with a quotation from Maxine Hong Kingston's *The Woman Warrior*? If you have read the selection from "Tongue-Tied" (NR 381, SE 230), this question should produce discussion on the similarity of the two writers' concerns. It should also lead students to see that a writer surrenders his or her voice to another *only* when that other writer's words are so powerful that they cannot be avoided— or to put it another way, quote only when summary or paraphrase won't do the trick.

2. Why does Mairs arrange her three rules in the order she does? Why is it relevant that she uses an "if" formulation for rules 2 and 3?

3. What examples follow each rule? Why does Mairs limit the number of examples?

4. According to Mairs, men are always telling women to "lighten up," to show a sense of humor (Paragraph 10). How and where does Mairs reveal a sense of humor? Why does she sometimes choose to be deadly earnest?

5. The essay ends swiftly, with two brief paragraphs. How does Mairs provide a sense of conclusion through her style? Why does Mairs end with a question?

Suggested Writing Assignments

1. Before listing her three rules, Mairs writes, "If, in a fit of wishful thinking, you're inclined to dismiss them as passé, spend a few hours in the classrooms or corridors of a coeducational high school or college"(paragraph 3). Do just what Mairs suggests and report your findings in an essay that either supports or challenges Mairs'

2. Mairs suggests that discourse among women is a study of its own—and, by implication, that discourse among men is another such study. Observe the language of women (or men) in single-sex groups, and write an essay about it—perhaps comparing it with the behavior Mairs describes in her essay.
3. Have the language patterns between men and women changed from your parents' generation to your own? After observing groups from both generations, write an essay in response to this question.

LEWIS THOMAS

Notes on Punctuation

The Norton Reader, p. 395; Shorter Edition, p. 249

"Notes on Punctuation" provides a lighthearted and witty supplement to classwork on punctuation. Thomas' conversational tone and obvious delight in learning give life to the arguably dry topic of punctuation. His "rules" are likely to be remembered longer than any grammar handbook's prescription, for they are simple, personal, and logical. Students might find it interesting that Thomas is a science writer, not an English teacher—and you might refer them to his other essays in *The Norton Reader:* "The Long Habit" (NR 247, SE 136) and "On Magic in Medicine" (NR 483, SE 296).

Analytical Considerations

1. What is the difference between the comma, semicolon, and period, on the one hand, and the question mark and exclamation point, on the other? How does Thomas communicate this difference?
2. In one sentence, summarize Thomas' sense of the purpose and value of punctuation. Why is Thomas' essay more effective in making this point than a single sentence can be?
3. Ask students to evaluate Thomas' opening and closing paragraphs. Do they detract from the serious points Thomas makes in many places in the essay? Why or why not?
4. Thomas writes particularly good paragraphs, for they conform to the traditional principles of unity, coherence, and emphasis. Ask students to analyze, for instance, paragraph 2 or paragraph 5.
5. Thomas' tone is especially important in treating this potentially dry

topic. Discuss some places where his wit and personality come through (paragraphs 2, 5, and 9, for example) and work toward a description of his persona. In the end what makes this an interesting and engaging essay?

6. Does Thomas really believe there are "no precise rules about punctuation"?

Suggested Writing Assignments

1. Select a favorite essay in *The Norton Reader,* and analyze its author's use of commas, semicolons, and exclamation points according to Thomas' guidelines. Turn your analysis into an essay on punctuation.

2. Test Thomas' principles for punctuation on several poems. Write an essay on your discoveries.

3. Do you agree with Thomas that "the essential flavor of language . . . is its wonderful ambiguity" (paragraph 1)? Elaborate on or disagree with Thomas' point in an essay.

4. Apply the principles of punctuation set forth here to Thomas' other two essays in *The Norton Reader.* Analyze each, then write an essay on whether or not Thomas has lived up to his own principles. Do his views on punctuation suggest a more general stance toward his subject and his audience that contributes to his success as an essayist?

Additional questions on this essay will be found in the text (NR 397–98, SE 251–52).

WAYNE C. BOOTH

Boring from Within: The Art of the Freshman Essay

The Norton Reader, p. 405; Shorter Edition, p. 252

Although Booth focuses on how to teach students to write well, his ultimate objective is to guide students to think for themselves. Booth views his two aims—good writing and cogent thinking—as complementary; only "thinking boys and girls" will write papers that aren't boring or in other ways frustrating. As he elucidates the problem of boring essays and potential remedies, Booth himself attempts to be not only organized and clear but also interesting and controversial.

Analytical Considerations

1. What is the occasion for Booth's address? How has this occasion helped to shape Booth's language, structure, and evidence?
2. How do paragraphs 5 and 6 set up the rest of this essay? Block off the essay into sections, and ask students to explain what Booth does in each section and how it functions as a part of the whole.
3. Are Booth's attacks on *Time* and *Newsweek* justified? Bring in recent issues—or ask your students to—in order to test the legitimacy of Booth's remarks.
4. Extract three principles for good writing from "Boring from Within." Then compare Booth's philosophy of composition with George Orwell's in "Politics and the English Language" (NR 417, SE 264). Would the two writers agree on these principles?
5. Point out examples of exaggeration and satiric humor in Booth's essay. Is the tone that these elements create geared to Booth's audience and thesis? Explain.
6. In light of some of his comments, would you call Booth an elitist? If so, what statements make him seem that way?

Suggested Writing Assignments

1. Read the op-ed page in the *New York Times* or another major newspaper for a week and select a column that is not boring. Analyze it and write an essay that explains why and how the writer succeeds in avoiding the pitfalls of being "boring from within."
2. Test the validity and accuracy of Booth's criticism of popular magazine journalism by reading several issues of *Time* or *Newsweek;* choose representative articles and write an analytical essay.
3. Select and write about a model of "genuine narration, with the sharp observation and penetrating critical judgment that underlies all good story telling" (paragraph 28).
4. Booth does not try to soft-pedal his criticism of typical freshman writing. Does this essay offend you as a student? Does it contain a fair assessment of students' abilities and productivity? Does it offer ideas that may help you to write better, more interesting essays? Write a closely argued response to "Boring from Within."
5. Booth seems to believe that there are topics that can personally engage almost any college student. These topics lie in the area of "social problems." Think of some topics that college freshmen

ought to be able to write interesting, controversial responses to. (You might do this as a class to make sure that the appeal of the topics is widespread.) Then individually write on one of the agreed-on topics and compare your essay with others from the class.

Additional questions on this essay will be found in the text (NR 416–16, SE 263–64).

GEORGE ORWELL

Politics and the English Language

The Norton Reader, p. 417; Shorter Edition, p. 264

This essay is one of the most famous on language and meaning, from one of the twentieth century's best English prose stylists. Because language is "not an instrument which we shape for our own purposes," Orwell assumes an active stance in seeking to purge the English language of errors, obfuscation, cant, and corruption. He does more than diagnose the illness; he offers a prescription that is practical, although not painless. Implied in the reform of the English language is the reform of political systems; for as far as Orwell is concerned, corruption in the use of language and corruption in politics are connected.

Analytical Considerations

1. Describe Orwell's goals and methods in "Politics and the English Language." Which methods do you find most effective?
2. What is the source of the good English that Orwell turns into "modern English of the worst sort"? Why does Orwell use this source to illustrate his point?
3. Does Orwell seem to lose his way in the first half of this essay, particularly after paragraphs 1 and 2 in which he discusses politics and language? Is his deliberate postponement of his analysis of the five writing samples an effective device?
4. Ask students to find and evaluate some of Orwell's metaphors. Are they fresh and lively? Are they dated or drawn from a cultural context too far removed from those of the students? Ask students which metaphors they find most powerful—and why.
5. Ask each student to summarize Orwell's essay by extracting six

statements that best represent the spirit and intention of the writer. Then ask students to compare their choices of the six statements. What does it mean that we, as readers, make so many of the same choices?

6. Ask students to bring in examples of the problems discussed by Orwell and to rewrite at least one passage for consideration in class.

Suggested Writing Assignments

1. Revise an essay written for this course by following Orwell's six rules.
2. If we are approaching an election year, find one of the countless speeches made by a politician. (The *New York Times* is a good place to look, because it is a newspaper of record.) Write an analysis of the speech you have chosen; base your analysis on Orwell's ideas in "Politics and the English Language."
3. Select another essay by Orwell and analyze it according to his principles and standards.
4. If you are using the regular *Norton Reader*, compare and contrast Orwell's rhetorical principles with those of H. L. Mencken in "Gamalielese" (NR 369).
5. Explain why, as Orwell asserts, "to think clearly is a necessary first step towards political regeneration" (paragraph 3). On the basis of what he says in "Thinking as a Hobby" (NR 181, SE 118), do you think William Golding would concur with Orwell's assertion?

Additional questions on this essay will be found in the text (NR 428, SE 275).

AN ALBUM OF STYLES

INTRODUCTION

What is style? The question defies an easy answer, especially if we accept the old adage "the style is the man." But if we can gain insight into a person's character by considering his or her actions, we can similarly work toward understanding a writer's style by examining the elements—the words, syntax, rhetorical techniques, and maneuvers—that create it. For the purposes of this unit, let's say that a writer's style is that personal, recognizable, and inseparable sense of the writer's self that permeates a text. It is the voice the reader hears—clear, distinct, and individual. It is not superfluous ornamentation or decorative afterthought, but the voiceprint of the writer that emerges from sustained practice and successive drafts of writing.

We can speak of different types of prose style—Renaissance or Augustan, baroque or plain style, for example—and isolate recurring features of each. At different times writers have subscribed to particular models of style, imitating qualities of sentence structure, word choice and usage, and tone. Jonathan Swift's dictum that "proper words, in proper places, make the style" may perhaps sound simplistic. Yet it is on target, for it is on this most basic level, the level of words, that style is built.

When we ask our students to talk about style, we need to give them some basic issues to ponder. Here are questions that may be of some help:

1. What kinds of words does the writer use? From what sources?
2. What types of sentences does the writer prefer?
3. What kinds of sentence patterns does the writer establish? Do the sentences have rhythm and balance or are they characterized by unusual, irregular rhythms?
4. What features of sound do you notice? Is alliteration an important element? Is assonance? How are such effects achieved?
5. Do repetition, variation, and contrast contribute to the prose?
6. Are there significant pauses in the text? How does the writer incorporate both pauses and silence?
7. What is the writer's characteristic tone? What kind of persona does he or she create?

You may want to add other questions. You might also encourage students to develop their own checklist for style. The key concern is that students begin to find ways to recognize and discuss the elements of style; reading, discussing, and writing about selections of noteworthy style can help students develop their own styles.

The classical tradition of imitating stylistic models can be helpful so long as students do not think that they must write in a certain style all the time. Perhaps read to them the passage in Benjamin Franklin's *Autobiography* in which he reads and imitates the essays of Addison and Steele—but suggest that Franklin both imitates and deviates. If you try imitation exercises, emphasize that these efforts are intended to help them discover their own styles, just as imitation helped Franklin. Acquiring style can be a slow process, but students can take some comfort in the words of Samuel Johnson on the subject: "What is written without effort is in general read without pleasure."

FRANCIS BACON

Of Revenge

The Norton Reader, p. 429; Shorter Edition, p. 276

Francis Bacon represents the English Renaissance style best termed "sententious," from the Latin *sententia,* meaning "a saying" or "maxim." Derived from classical models, this style is formal with its development achieved by metaphor and parallel constructions. The passage from Bacon should be read aloud to give full attention to how rhythm and balance work.

1. What kinds of sentences does Bacon use? Why?
2. What is the effect created by Bacon's references?
3. Characterize Bacon's word choice. What makes it seem "formal" to us? Would it have been in his day?
4. How does Bacon's use of punctuation differ from ours? Is it merely erratic, or does it mark a different sense of sentence construction?
5. Bacon's "Of Revenge" is printed as just one paragraph. Would it be paragraphed differently today? How?

JOHN DONNE

No Man Is an Island

The Norton Reader, p. 430; Shorter Edition, p. 227

This selection works well in conjunction with Northrop Frye's "The Motive for Metaphor" (NR 1055, SE 663) because it uses an extended metaphor or "conceit" so skillfully for homiletic purposes. Before (or while) discussing the passage, you might ask students how many of the phrases and sentences they have heard before. The familiarity of Donne's sermon reminds us that certain styles are more memorable and quotable than others.

1. How do we know that Francis Bacon and Donne studied similar, if not identical, rhetorical traditions?
2. Trace the development of metaphor in "No Man Is an Island."
3. How does Donne use transitional words? What is the effect of their logical claims?
4. What is the effect of the closing phrase: "it tolls for thee." How do the single syllable words contribute to this effect?

ABRAHAM LINCOLN

The Gettysburg Address

The Norton Reader, p. 433; Shorter Edition, p. 227

As legend has it, Abraham Lincoln's brief, moving address was scribbled on the back of an envelope. In fact, Lincoln's "Gettysburg Address," the result of considerable revision, transcends time and place as it illustrates the principles of clarity, economy, and elegance.

1. How many sentences has Lincoln written? Are they varied in type and length? Ask students to analyze and evaluate the effect of the last sentence.
2. Does Lincoln's speech show any traces of the classical rhetoric of Francis Bacon and John Donne?
3. Consider the impact that Lincoln achieves by repetition, not just of words but of constructions like prepositional phrases.

ERNEST HEMINGWAY

From *A Farewell to Arms*

The Norton Reader, p. 435; Shorter Edition, p. 278

Ernest Hemingway's style may be the most easily recognized in English prose, and this example is typical Hemingway: crisp, conversational, dominated by nouns and articles, filled with words of Anglo-Saxon derivation, free of Latinate influence, and developed by accumulation.

1. What kinds of words form Hemingway's writing vocabulary?
2. How does Hemingway use the conjunction *and* here? What kind of syntactical (and even philosophical) preference does it signal?
3. How and why are rhythm, balance, and parallel construction important to Hemingway?
4. What kind of relationship between writer and reader does Hemingway attempt to establish?
5. What adjectives would you attach to Hemingway's style?

VIRGINIA WOOLF

What the Novelist Gives Us

The Norton Reader, p. 436; Shorter Edition, p. 278

Here, in an essay from *The Second Common Reader*, Virginia Woolf provides advice on how to read a book. Woolf's style is informal, certainly conversational, yet it is also learned, distinguished by easy reference to a range of literary works only a well-read reader could appreciate.

Analytic Considerations

1. "What the Novelist Gives Us" seems to use a loose and discursive style. Is this style at odds with its content? Or is its rhetorical pose meant to establish rapport with the reader?
2. What is the function of reference to Daniel Defoe, Jane Austen, and Thomas Hardy in "What the Novelist Gives Us"? How do they create persona as well as provide content?

3. Why does Woolf use the second person *you* throughout this essay? What effect does it have?
4. Does Woolf include a thesis statement? Where?
5. Ask students how Woolf has organized her essay. Why, for example, does she not describe "what the novelist gives us" until the last sentence?
6. What is the most appropriate audience for this essay? Why?

Suggested Writing Assignments

1. Write an essay about what you expect books to give you.
2. Using several examples to illustrate your points, write an essay about how to read a novel.

E. B. WHITE

Progress and Change

The Norton Reader, p. 437; Shorter Edition, p. 280

Written fifty years ago, "Progress and Change" retains its communicative power because of E. B. White's insight into human beings and his ability to craft clear, hard-edged prose. This one-paragraph informal essay compresses sharp observation into forceful expression and invites comparison with Henry David Thoreau (for content) and Benjamin Franklin (for style).

Analytical Considerations

1. Ask students to analyze the first sentence as a rhetorical strategy.
2. This paragraph could be broken into two paragraphs. Ask students where and why. Then let them speculate about why White chose not to do so.
3. Ask students what White's purpose is. Are they persuaded by the argument of "Progress and Change"? Do they accept White's assertion that there is "a dim degeneracy in progress"?
4. Ask students what would be an appropriate context for this essay as a spoken presentation. What features of a spoken style does this written essay retain?
5. All of White's writing is distinguished by his use of concrete, sometimes homely, matter-of-fact details. Some are metaphors,

others analogies, but all are important to the style as well as the content of White's writing. On that basis, compare "Progress and Change" with "Democracy" (NR 934, SE 572).
6. Read and discuss "Once More to the Lake" (NR 55, SE 47) as an essay on "progress and change."
7. The styles of Virginia Woolf and White could both be called "conversational." How are they alike and different in their sense of conversation?

Suggested Writing Assignments

1. Write your own essay on progress and change. Limit yourself to one paragraph, and try writing 500 to 750 words on the subject.
2. Write an essay in response to White's observation that "there is always a subtle danger in life's refinements, a dim degeneracy in progress."

WILLIAM FAULKNER

Nobel Prize Award Speech

The Norton Reader, p. 438; Shorter Edition, p. 281

William Faulkner's speech, written in what some would consider a ponderous and self-impressed tone, provides a useful opportunity to focus on how "occasion" influences a writer's style. Have students compare their responses to Faulkner's speech and Virginia Woolf's "What the Novelist Gives Us" (NR 436, SE 278) or "In Search of a Room of Own's Own" (NR, 1111, SE 707) to explore this question.
1. What kinds of words does Faulkner use? Why?
2. Study the structure and patterns of Faulkner's sentences. Read the first paragraph aloud, then discuss its effects, rhythmical and otherwise. Has Faulkner used sentence variation effectively?
3. What is the purpose of Faulkner's use of "Our" in "Our tragedy" (paragraph 2)? What is he trying to do? Is he successful?
4. Characterize the tone of this speech.

JAMES THURBER

A Dog's Eye View of Man

The Norton Reader, p. 439; Shorter Edition, p. 282

This is a neat satirical piece from a masterful humorist. Because humor is one of the salient features of James Thurber's style, it might be wise to ask how he creates and uses humor.
1. Why does Thurber capitalize *Man*?
2. How has Thurber determined his paragraphs?
3. What is the point of "A Dog's Eye View of Man"?
4. How is the style inseparable from the content?

JOHN UPDIKE

Beer Can

The Norton Reader, p. 440; Shorter Edition, p. 283

John Updike's well-known reflection on a beer can is not the lighthearted short piece it first seems. Rather, it is a serious reflection on social and cultural change, cleverly focused on a mundane object. It invites comparison with E. B. White's "Progress and Change" (NR 437, SE 280).
1. How do the opening and closing sentences frame this essay? How do they differ from the intervening sentences? Why?
2. How does Updike involve his reader in this paragraph?
3. Does Updike achieve specificity by the same means as White?
4. How, in its style as well as its content, is "Beer Can" a cultural document?

D. KEITH MANO

How to Keep from Getting Mugged

The Norton Reader, p. 441; Shorter Edition, p. 283

D. Keith Mano's piece uses the language of the streets—as he gives advice for surviving in an urban environment. Language, as

Mano suggests, can be a form of protection or self-defense. Written in 1982, the piece will seem both relevant and dated to students of the 1990s. You might use it to discuss how street slang changes yet how, through Mano's style, we still continue to get its message.

1. Why is Mano's primary sentence mode the imperative? To whom is he giving advice—his readers or himself?
2. What words or phrases have gone out of vogue? Do such changes affect our ability to understand Mano's writing?
3. From what sources besides street slang does Mano draw his language? What is the effect of these multiple sources?
4. Not all of Mano's sentences are sentences. Why? What affect does he intend?
5. Study Mano's punctuation. How does it contribute to the style of the piece?

Suggested Writing Assignments

1. Write a paragraph or two in deliberate imitation of one writer from this section.
2. Enter any selection from this section into a computer system programmed to revise and improve texts. Compare and contrast the original and new texts. What has been gained? What has been lost? Write an essay about this experiment in style.
3. Consider all selections in the order presented, and write an essay about the evolution of English prose style from Bacon to Mano.

SIGNS OF THE TIMES

ANTHONY BURGESS

Is America Falling Apart?

The Norton Reader, p. 443; Shorter Edition, p. 285

Anthony Burgess, an Englishman (as he makes clear in the course of this essay), offers an outsider's response to its title question, "Is America Falling Apart?" You might ask students how they think Burgess acquired the authority (in 1971, when he spent his year in America) to estimate that nearly 50 percent "of the entire American population" think that their country is "coming apart at the seams" (paragraph 21); whom did he talk to, and what did they tell him? Research and documentation are not among the virtues of his essay. Nor is precision: when he describes the personal experience that serves as evidence for his strictures on America, he situates himself, vaguely, in New Jersey. Where in New Jersey? Newark? Princeton? Ho Ho Kus? It would make a difference. You might ask students to reconstruct Burgess' year in America on the evidence he provides in this essay.

Burgess' essay is loosely connected. Although individual paragraphs are coherent and bear some relation to his title question, the connections between them are as often associative as consecutive. He divides the essay into five sections by spacing: paragraphs 1 through 5, 6 through 8, 9 through 12, 14 through 18, and 19 through 21. Do these spatial divisions mark units within the essay? Since they really don't, except in the most impressionistic of ways, what then is their function? You might also call students' attention to Burgess' reversal at the end of the essay (paragraph 21), in which he owns that he finds America "more stimulating than depressing" and expects to return. Does he prepare for this reversal in the course of the essay or is it something of a surprise?

Students will probably need to be encouraged to pull apart an essay by a professional writer and see how many of the principles of "good" writing they dutifully learn *can* be, and at times *should* be, violated. They probably will have been engaged by Burgess' essay; if they haven't been, or won't admit that they have been, then you'll have to dramatize your own engagement. You might turn the discussion to the differences between having an opinion and being opinionated. Opinionated people can be boring and tedious; Burgess isn't, and that's what makes him worth reading.

Analytical Considerations

1. Burgess' exaggerations, such as his assured estimate of the percentage of Americans who agree with him, fall under a technique called hyperbole. You might ask students to identify other hyperboles in the essay and consider their effect. How do the frequent hyperboles characterize Burgess? What kind (or kinds) of responses do they elicit from readers? In what kinds of writing is it legitimate to use hyperbole, in what kinds illegitimate?
2. Ask students to identify some of Burgess' criticisms of America that they find valid. Do they find them valid in Burgess' own terms or by toning down his hyperbole?

Suggested Writing Assignments

1. Write an opinionated essay of your own in answer to some provocative question.
2. Burgess describes Americans as guilty and masochistic, eager to confess their national faults and accept blame for them (paragraph 13). Write an essay in which you play this kind of American. (You might, in a coda, discuss whether this kind of role playing is easy or difficult for you.)
3. Burgess calls America "a revolutionary republic based on a romantic view of human nature" (paragraph 20) and refers to the "dangerous naiveté of The Declaration of Independence" (paragraph 12). Read the final version of "The Declaration of Independence" (NR 928, SE 567) in conjunction with these statements, try to reconstruct his reading of the document, and respond with your own.

Additional questions on this essay will be found in the text (NR 449, SE 291).

ADA LOUISE HUXTABLE

Modern-Life Battle: Conquering Clutter

The Norton Reader, p. 450; Shorter Edition, p. 292

Ada Louise Huxtable, now an editor of the *New York Times,* was formerly its architecture critic. In this essay, however, she displays her professional knowledge about the history of interior decoration and its sociological significance. The focus of the essay is the wit and cleverness with which she looks at other people's houses. Students should note the magisterial classificatory statement with which she opens the essay—all the world is divided into two sorts of people, those horrified by vacuums and those horrified by the things that fill them—and her subsequent reduction of it to domestic interiors. She modifies this scheme with a third category, calculated clutter, and then introduces another large distinction, those who are not in control of clutter (and presumably those who are). Not until this point in the essay does she acknowledge her personal involvement, and only briefly: She returns to her detached analysis, enlivened by a keen eye and a witty analysis of what she sees. It may be worth spending time getting students to hear Huxtable's tonal variations though you choose not to.

Students should be able to reconstruct from this essay a number of the classificatory schemes that undergird it. These are the styles of interior decoration, these are the rooms that exemplify them. These are some rooms I have seen; this is how I read them—sociologically and psychologically—with respect to the motives of their owners. Formally presented, these schemes can be labeled either deductive, beginning with categories and finding examples, or inductive, beginning with rooms and sorting them into categories. In Huxtable's essay they are not quite either: Such schemes are incompatible with its personal and idiosyncratic tone.

Analytical Considerations

1. To look at Huxtable's tonal variations, start with a sentence like "Really living without clutter takes an iron will, plus a certain stoicism about the little comforts of life" (paragraph 5). You might describe the poles of style as overgeneral and overparticular, or as

magisterial and cozy. Ask students, individually or in groups, to find other examples of witty juxtapositions of tone.

2. If class discussion of Huxtable's classificatory schemes seems profitable, you might ask students to reconstruct one or more of those that undergird her essay both deductively and inductively and to explain them in writing, to see what tone the formal use of classificatory schemes leads them to adopt.

Suggested Writing Assignments

1. Divide the world into two kinds of people, as Huxtable does, and write an essay, witty or serious, in which you follow through your initial classificatory scheme.
2. Establish a classificatory scheme with respect to some aspect of contemporary life and then write an essay in which you blur it in order to create a personal voice and an individual response.
3. Write an essay in which, as a neutral observer and potential sociologist and psychologist, you describe a particular room and "read" its sociological and psychological import.
4. Take a room whose inhabitants you know and write the kind of essay about it described in Suggested Writing Assignment 3, in which you disguise the source of your knowledge and your involvement, or in which you use your knowledge and your involvement, or both.

Additional questions on this essay will be found in the text (NR 453–54, SE 295–96).

LEWIS THOMAS

On Magic in Medicine

The Norton Reader, p. 483; Shorter Edition, p. 296

In this essay Lewis Thomas, a medical doctor, researcher, and administrator-turned-essayist, assumes the role of a "skeptic in medicine." He uses as his central text a Blue Cross advertisement for "Seven Healthy Life Habits" and critically analyzes the epidemiological study from which the advertisement's seven prescriptions are derived (paragraphs 9 through 13). Students should attend carefully to his discussion of cause-and-effect relationships (paragraphs 9 and 10) and their reversibility. Epidemiological studies claim only correlations. But a gullible public will, so Blue Cross hopes, take them as proof that they ought to alter their habits, whether or not they actually do, and ought to feel guilty if they don't.

Analytical Considerations

1. You might look closely with students at Thomas' account of the epidemiological study from which the Blue Cross advertisement is derived: It is a lucid explanation of technical information. Students should notice how Thomas sorts and groups the seven precepts and gets simpler explanations out of the way before turning to more difficult ones.
2. Look at the range of material Thomas uses to frame and buttress his reading of the Blue Cross advertisement, from the history of medicine to the contemporary scene. Ask students to distinguish between what is unfamiliar and what is familiar to them. Are Thomas' explanations underspecific, overspecific, or about right? Do they think he had readers like themselves in mind as he wrote?
3. Consider the personal elements in Thomas' essay. Are they necessary to his diagnosis of Americans' gullibility with respect to diseases and cures? What do they contribute?

Suggested Writing Assignments

1. Locate and use as your central text an advertisement for a self-help book: the *New York Times Book Review* invariably advertises books that promise to teach you, for example, how to lose weight, how to have a good sex life, or how to succeed on the job. Write an essay in which you frame your text to elucidate "folk doctrine" about the subject of the advertisement and self-help in general.
2. Do library research on what is called "iatrogenic disease," or disease induced by doctors. Write an essay in which you explain it with examples and consider it in relation to the attitudes about diseases and cures that Thomas discusses.
3. Compare Thomas' account of Americans' gullibility with Stephen Jay Gould's account, in "The Terrifying Normalcy of Aids" (NR 702, SE 424), of their false confidence in technological fixes. What elements of information and interpretation are common to their essays? How does each author situate himself in relation to his material and to his audience?

Additional questions on this essay will be found in the text (NR486–87, SE 300).

JOHN McMURTRY

Kill 'Em! Crush 'Em! Eat 'Em Raw!

The Norton Reader, p. 454; Shorter Edition, p. 300

John McMurtry, a Canadian professor of philosophy, has written an essay about his experiences as a professional football player. He moves smoothly from personal report to impersonal generalization. He starts in the present, with the flaring up of an old injury, and moves back to his love of athletics, the increasing professionalization of his participation in sports, and the injuries that finally led him to quit the game. He then broadens his scope to consider the social role of professional sports, particularly violent and damaging ones like football.

Although his arguments for and against professional sports may seem familiar, indeed overrehearsed, McMurtry derives his authority from his unusual career as both player and philosopher. He condemns professional football, but judiciously. Perhaps what is most engaging about his essay is his depiction of himself as a player caught up in the ethos of the sport, accepting its rules and hazards with some sense of disquiet but without much questioning.

Analytical Considerations

1. You might ask students to consider the various dimensions of McMurtry's overarching analogy between football and war. What claims about football does the analogy make? And, conversely, what claims about war? Are both sets of claims acceptable to them?
2. Herb Goldberg, in "In Harness: The Male Condition" (NR 509, SE 307), argues that men are imprisoned by "traditional definitions of masculine-appropriate behavior" (paragraph 13). To what extent do these definitions figure in McMurtry's account?

Suggested Writing Assignments

1. Perhaps you have found yourself in a situation similar to McMurtry's, participating in an activity that later you decide you should not have participated in or did not want to participate in. Write an essay in which you reconstruct your state of mind during your participation and the process that led you to change your mind about participation and/or to give it up.

2. Critics from a number of spheres are calling into question the professionalization of sports on college campuses. What is the status of sports on your campus? Write an essay in which you argue for their lesser or greater professionalization.
3. Write an essay in which you consider why becoming a professional athlete should be so attractive to some men or to some women. You can develop your essay through experience or research. If your own experience or the experience of a friend is relevant, use it. Or do library research on a particular professional athlete.

Additional questions on this essay will be found in the text (NR 460, SE 306–07).

HERB GOLDBERG

In Harness: The Male Condition

The Norton Reader, p. 509; Shorter Edition, p. 307

Goldberg is a psychologist, professor, and writer. "In Harness: The Male Condition" bears the marks of his therapeutic practice. It begins with a long example, a case study of a man who was probably his patient. Then, after generalizing about the male condition, Goldberg includes three vignettes, obtained by a request that these men (who may or may not have been his patients) write to him: the forty-six-year-old businessman, the thirty-nine-year-old carpenter, and the fifty-seven-year-old college professor (paragraphs 26 to 29). The fourth vignette is his own: at thirty-five he devoted himself to his family and at fifty-seven he feels unrewarded. What is the effect of this delay in Goldberg's announcing his own involvement with his subject? While Goldberg includes individual cases to illustrate his generalizations, when he generalizes he speaks of men, collectively, as if gender unites them more than other circumstances—large circumstances of social and economic class, of race and ethnicity and small circumstances of infinite variety—divide them. He creates a universal that may well be false. A similar error is often charged to the women's movement. Goldberg on the one hand argues that the women's movement offers men little in achieving their own liberation; on the other hand, he is clearly aware of the movement as a model both to emulate and to react against.

Analytical Considerations

1. Given Goldberg's clinical, detached presentation, his delayed announcing his own involvement with his subject (and perhaps with his patients' predicaments) may be misleading. Be sure to make the point that personal involvement itself is not the problem: Students are too often caught up in the notion that clinical detachment is better, truer. The problem is Goldberg's detached presentation and tone.
2. Sigmund Freud asked a much-quoted question with respect to women: What do women want? Get your students to ask Goldberg (at least as he is represented in this essay): What do men want? He's more articulate about their discontents than their contents. Apparently what he wants for himself is to research, publish, teach, administer, play tennis, and travel.

Suggested Writing Assignments

1. Write an essay in which you analyze Goldberg's construction of a false universal. What characteristics do the individual men included in his essay share? What characteristics individualize them? Suggest some additional characteristics that need to be included for him to speak to and for a more representative, if still not universal, group of men.
2. Androgyny is a condition in which both male and female qualities are incorporated and valued. Does Goldberg see the liberation of men as their becoming androgynous? Are there characteristics of women he would like to appropriate for them? Are there characteristics of women he would not like to appropriate for them? Write an essay on the role of androgyny in Goldberg's thought.

Additional questions on this essay will be found in the text (NR 514–15, SE 312–13).

GLORIA STEINEM

The Good News Is: These Are Not the Best Years of Your Life

The Norton Reader, p. 515; Shorter Edition, p. 313

This essay first appeared in *Ms.* magazine, of which Steinem was a founder, in 1979. Steinem asks a question she is now ready to answer, why younger women, college-age women in particular, are not actively feminist. The genre of her essay is persuasion, and of a particular sort: she not only wants readers to understand her position but also to understand why once she believed something else and then changed her mind. Taking a second look, she not only questions her mistaken beliefs but also looks at the false expectations and assumptions that underlay them.

The structure of the essay is well marked. After describing her former beliefs, she turns to what she believes now. "Consider a few of the reasons," she concludes paragraph 3: in paragraphs 4 through 15 she considers the contemporary scene; paragraphs 16 to 18, the first and second women's movements, regularly devoting one paragraph to developing and explaining each reason. Then she concludes with the inverse of what her present position implies: If college-age women are not actively feminist, older women are.

Women students, both younger and older, may or may not accept Steinem's view of their lives; they may also need to be reminded that Steinem, rather than criticizing them, explains and excuses them. Moreover, the developmental scheme she traces in their lives she sees as present in her own (paragraph 3).

Women students may or may not be willing to talk about this developmental scheme, although older women are usually more willing to talk about such things than younger women. Men students may be only too willing to talk about the pressures on them. At some point you will probably want to turn the discussion back to the false assumptions that Steinem sees underlying her former views: single-sex models of cultural patterns, including, in this essay, human development and revolution.

Analytical Considerations

1. You might refer students to "'Generic' *He*" (G p. 66) and ask them to distinguish between verbal false generics and conceptual false

generics. You might also ask them to read Casey Miller and Kate Swift, "Who's in Charge of the English Language?" (NR 363, SE 241) for a discussion of how language creates our concepts.

2. Steinem creates four categories to describe college-age women's responses to feminism (paragraph 15). Discuss the adequacy of her classificatory scheme. You might also ask students to imagine this scheme, which appears in a minor way in Steinem's essay, as the organizing scheme of another essay. What kind of essay would it be?

3. Particularly if you've had students analyze Herb Goldberg's construction of a false universal—see "In Harness: The Male Condition" (NR 509, SE 307; Suggested Writing Assignment 1)— you will want to have them look at Steinem's qualification with respect to women: "every generalization based on female culture has many exceptions" (paragraph 3). Is this qualification sufficient to exempt her from constructing a false universal about women?

Suggested Writing Assignments

1. Take a second look: Write an essay in which you look at something you've changed your mind about, accounting for what you used to believe, what you believe now, and how you changed your mind.

2. Steinem claims a "depth of feminist change" on campus that observers often miss. Assemble what evidence of change you can, through your own experience and by interviewing at least one woman of another generation. Depending on who you interview, you can compare the present with a past of ten, twenty, thirty, or even more years ago.

3. Carol Gilligan's *In a Different Voice* (1982) is an extended study of a single-sex model of moral development. Read it and write a brief essay in which you explain Gilligan's theory of how single-sex cultural patterns affect women.

BETTY ROLLIN

Motherhood: Who Needs It?

The Norton Reader, p. 521; Shorter Edition, p. 319

Although Betty Rollin never says so, the answer to her question "Who needs motherhood?" is "Nobody." This essay, written in 1970 for *Look,* a mass-circulation magazine now defunct, still generates strong responses. Virtually all students disagree with her argument and object to the tough way she argues; very few admit even to enjoying the essay. It's hard for them to imagine anyone taking her uncompromising position and calculatedly choosing to antagonize readers.

What students need to see is that Rollin makes her case against motherhood like a debater: She illustrates her argument with clear cut evidence—no one she quotes has anything good to say about motherhood—and apparently she is out to win. If she brings up counterarguments, she dismisses them as propaganda and brainwashing. But does she really expect us to agree with her position? Think of a debate. The case *for* motherhood has been made often enough, as strongly and with as little qualification as Rollins makes the case *against* it. In place of all the goo that has been spread on the subject, Rollins throws acid. Somewhere between goo and acid must lie a reasonable view.

Analytical Considerations

1. Ask students, individually or in groups to, look at Rollins' language, particularly at her exaggerated, frequently outrageous statements (or hyperboles). Can they hear her as quotable and appreciate the wit of her formulations?
2. You might ask students to consider their antagonistic response to Rollin as gender based. Do they identify argument and debate as male, persuasion as female? Is a tough style legitimate for men, illegitimate for women?
3. Direct students to paragraphs 30 through 32, the last three paragraphs of Rollin's essay. How are they different from the rest of the essay? Why do they think she included them?

Suggested Writing Assignments

1. Write a debater's argument against some generally revered custom or institution. You might try "Fatherhood: Who Needs It?"
2. Try thinking of "Motherhood: Who Needs It?" as an example of sustained irony. Write an essay in which you compare it with Jonathan Swift's "A Modest Proposal" (NR 878, SE 522). Consider how both Swift and Rollin may be seen as creating a putative author who offers proposals that violate feelings.

Additional questions on this essay will be found in the text (NR 531–32, SE 329–30).

BRENT STAPLES

Black Men and Public Space

The Norton Reader, p. 550; Shorter Edition, p. 330

In this short essay Brent Staples writes about himself as an individual and as a universal, that is, as a well-educated and nonviolent black man who, by virtue of his gender and race, is perceived as belonging to a class: violent black men. He is not unsympathetic to women who avoid him on the streets at night: "the danger they perceive is not a hallucination." The essay provides an account of his initiation into awareness and his attempts to distinguish himself from other members of his putative class.

"Black Men and Public Space" is an episodic narrative with commentary. You might call students' attention to the four times and places of the essay—childhood in Pennsylvania; graduate school in Chicago; Chicago in the late 1970s and early 1980s; New York City now—and how Staples manipulates chronology. You might also want them to notice how the particularized narrative of the opening, that is, his first encounter with a "victim" as a graduate student in Chicago, reverberates against his more generalized narrative of other times and places.

Analytical Considerations

1. You might ask students to distinguish between narrative and commentary in this essay—and to notice how Staples combines

them. Whereas many essays frame personal experience with generalizing commentary, Staples' does not. Yet it is more than a personal report: It calls attention to larger problems.

2. The pressure of the unspoken in this essay generates irony. Students might consider verbal irony, such as Staples' describing the woman he encountered in Chicago as his *victim*, and dramatic irony, such as his whistling Vivaldi and Beethoven when he walks the streets late at night. Another irony would be Staples' "solution": his precautions against being taken for a mugger and a rapist. Are they really a solution? How does the unspoken exert pressure? What are the advantages and disadvantages of irony in this essay?

Suggested Writing Assignments

1. Rewrite Staples' essay as an unironic indictment of America as a racist society.
2. Write a personal essay about your experience of reading (and discussing) "Black Men and Public Space."
3. A longer version of "Black Men and Public Space" appeared in the September 1986 issue of *Ms.* magazine as "Just Walk on By." Read it and write an analysis of it in which you focus on two things: the relation of "Black Men and Public Space" (excerpted for *Harper's* magazine) to the longer "Just Walk on By" and the question of audience in both essays. How does Staples engage with his presumably different readers in each essay?

Additional questions on this essay will be found in the text (NR 553, SE 333).

SHELBY STEELE

The Recoloring of Campus Life

The Norton Reader, p. 554; Shorter Edition, p. 334

In "The Recoloring of Campus Life," Shelby Steele, a professor of English at San Jose State College in California, addresses a volatile and controversial subject: race relations and affirmative action on college campuses. Whether or not you decide to have students read and discuss it will depend on the situation on your campus and the composition and dynamics of your class. The essay was published in *Harper's* magazine in 1989; that is, it wasn't written with student readers in mind. Nevertheless, it is exemplary in Steele's judicious evenhandedness and careful assumption of authority. You will probably get around to noticing its firm structure: Steele presents his credentials, explains how he gathered his evidence, and then divides his presentation of it—black students speak, then white students speak—before presenting his own proposal for a politics of commonality rather than a politics of difference. Although he has a proposal, the essay is not primarily an argument for it: Steele devotes more attention to analyzing the social and psychological dynamics of campus unrest. But the structure of the essay is not where to begin class discussion.

Students will probably begin it themselves—after all, when someone generalizes about a group of which you are a member, your first response is, is this true of me? The question of constructing universals has surfaced in other essays in this section: Herb Goldberg's "In Harness: The Male Condition" (NR 509, SE 307) and in Gloria Steinem's "The Good News Is: These Are Not the Best Years of Your Life" (NR 515, SE 313). You might consider it in discussing Steele's essay as well. Has Steele constructed false universals—black students, white students? How might he construct true universals? How much qualification would be necessary? Is the entire enterprise of constructing universals doomed to fail? You will probably need to remind students that talk about groups rather than individuals is characteristic of academic disciplines other than literature: It is something they can expect to hear a lot of and do a lot of in college. Perhaps, then, universals are most problematic when we write about contemporary issues, when we read individuals, as the title of this section of *The Norton Reader* suggests, as signs of the times.

Analytic Considerations

1. Steele tends to heighten what he sees as paradoxes: for example, "I think racial tension on campus is the result more of racial equality than inequality" (paragraph 6). You might ask students to consider his evidence and his formulation of it as a paradox by the use of antithesis: equality versus inequality. They should be able to locate other instances of paradoxical formulations in the essay.
2. How does Steele incorporate personal experience into his analysis and to what ends? Would he argue its importance as strongly as

Paul Fussell does in "Thank God for the Atom Bomb" (NR 711, SE 433)?

Suggested Writing Assignments

1. Is this—that is, Steele's construction of a group to which I belong by virtue of my race—true of me? Write a private journal entry (for yourself), a semiprivate journal entry (to be shared with the class), and a public essay (to be read by an audience that does not know you) in response to this question.
2. Steele refers in a note to an earlier essay of his also published in *Harper's* magazine: "I'm Black, You're White, Who's Innocent? Race and Power in an Era of Blame" (footnote 2). The title suggests that he treats at greater length the theme of innocence that appears in "The Recoloring of Campus Life." Read it and write an essay in which you discuss its relation to the later essay, in analysis and in stance: Does Steele demonstrate similar evenhandedness and careful assumption of authority, and how?

Additional questions on this essay will be found in the text (NR 566, SE 346).

RUSSELL BAKER

Surely Not Cigar-Shaped!

The Norton Reader, p. 460; Shorter Edition, p. 346

Russell Baker's complaint that weather forecasts are no longer what they used to be requires age, experience, and attentiveness simply to understand. If you have laboriously to explain it, your students aren't going to find it funny. What, for example, does Baker have in mind when he speaks of "those cruel, pointed teeth" (paragraph 13)? Fortunately, newspapers still carry the old-fashioned weather maps that Baker yearns for; perhaps bringing photocopies of one to class will help to explain the essay to students who rely exclusively on television for their weather forecasts. Baker wrote this essay for the op-ed page of the *New York Times* in the summer of 1987, an extraordinarily hot summer that broke all records. Its theme, that things aren't what they used to be, may suggest an assignment—

perhaps an informal, in-class assignment—in which students turn their hands to their own comic yearnings for the good old days.

Suggested Writing Assignments

1. Write an essay about the good old days in which you describe and reflect on some pleasant aspect of the past now gone.
2. Alternatively, interview older family members about some aspect of the part they miss in the modern world. Write an essay in which you both report and analyze what you have learned.

NATURE AND THE ENVIRONMENT

ROBERT FINCH

Being at Two with Nature

The Norton Reader, p. 567; Shorter Edition, p. 349

Robert Finch is, by vocation and avocation, a nature writer, coeditor of *The Norton Book of Nature Writing* and author of such works as *Common Ground: A Naturalist's Cape Cod* (1981) and *Outlands: Journeys to the Outer Edges of Cape Cod* (1986). In this essay Finch tries to articulate what makes "nature writing" distinct from other related forms, such as scientific research or environmental advocacy. For him it is the "fundamental connection," almost mysterious, that nature writers see between human identity and the physical and biological world.

Although this essay opens the section on "Nature and the Environment," some instructors might prefer to assign it last, after students have read several examples of nature writing. If you assign it first, you might use it to prepare students for the various modes of writing they will encounter in this unit—meditative and philosophical, objective and observational, impassioned and argumentative—and for the fundamental question Finch raises: Why is reading and writing about nature so important to us as human beings? If you assign the essay last, you might use the students' reading experience as a way of testing—and challenging—Finch's notions about what nature writing is. Do nature writers, as Finch claims, have "no agenda—no theory to test, no point to prove"? Or do nature writers have an "agenda," but one presented in nonargumentative modes?

Analytical Considerations

1. "Being at Two with Nature" might be called an essay of definition in that Finch attempts to define "nature writing," its features and its purpose. Yet Finch begins with a series of personal memories. What function do they serve?
2. What alternative terms to "nature writing" does Finch suggest? Why does he choose this term?
3. Why does Finch return to the facts about wind midway through his essay? How does the recurrence of these facts aid both the structure

and content of the essay?

4. Where does Finch come closest to giving a definition of nature writing? How does he distinguish it from other forms?

5. What is the purpose of the final section of the essay (beginning "If the underlying intent of the genre . . . " in paragraph 19)? Ask students to plot the movement of the essay, from personal reminiscence to philosophical speculation.

Suggested Writing Assignments

1. In paragraph 14, Finch makes a distinction between "nature" and "environmental" writers, claiming that the former have "no agenda—no theory to test, no point to prove." Do one of the following:

   A. Use Finch's distinction to compare two essays in this section, one an example of "nature" writing, the other of "environmental" writing. Does Finch's distinction hold? Are there other significant points of comparison?

   B. Choose an example of nature writing that does not seem to fit Finch's definition; use it to formulate your own definition of what nature writing is.

2. Read one of the longer works of nature writing listed in paragraph 8, and write an essay in which you discuss the writer's "agenda" or purpose.

GRETEL EHRLICH

Spring

The Norton Reader, p. 574; Shorter Edition, p. 356

Gretel Ehrlich is a much-admired nature writer from Wyoming, the author of essays (*The Solace of Open Spaces*, 1985), poetry (*To Touch the Water*, 1981), and fiction (*Heart Mountain*, 1988 and *Drinking Dry Clouds*, 1991). "Spring," perhaps the most difficult essay in the "Nature" section, represents Ehrlich's attempt to come to terms with what spring means—to her personally and more universally to the human race.

Students may find it easiest to discuss the personal narratives Ehrlich embeds within the essay: her bout with pneumonia and her use of spring as a metaphor for recovery; her discovery of an injured eagle and the personal significance she attaches to its survival; the proposal of marriage from Joel, his death in a pickup accident, and her spring-inspired dream of his riding across the range on "a black studhorse." In each of these episodes Ehrlich sees the restorative power of the natural cycle, spring following winter. It is also important to ask, however, why Ehrlich includes details about time in Julius Caesar's reign and discussions with physicists about the illusoriness of human concepts: What is the significance of an Einsteinian concept of time in which past, present, and future become meaningless notions? You might ask whether Ehrlich successfully blend these different concepts of time, whether they stand in opposition to each other, or whether she finally privileges one over another.

Analytical Considerations

1. In paragraph 3, Ehrlich writes, "It's spring again and I wasn't finished with winter." How does the opening of her essay reflect this reluctance to come to terms with spring?
2. What does spring mean to Ehrlich? You might ask students to find places where Ehrlich uses metaphorical language to get at its significance. Why does Ehrlich rely on metaphors? Does any single metaphor capture spring's essence?
3. Why does Ehrlich include discussions of time—time in Julius Caesar's reign, Einsteinian time, cyclical time?
4. This essay works by association as much as by logical progression. Ask students to plot out the movement of the essay, trying to explain what each section achieves.
5. How does Ehrlich create a sense of unity? You might ask students to look for details—like the conversation with the physicist or the injured eagle—that keep recurring.
6. What is the significance of Ehrlich's ending—the dream of Joel riding a black horse north across the range? Does it successfully bring together the various strands of "Spring"?

Suggested Writing Assignments

1. Write you own essay about spring and its significance to you.
2. Write about another season by blending your own experiences with meanings that human beings have traditionally attached to the season you've chosen.

DAVID RAINS WALLACE

The Mind of the Beaver

The Norton Reader, p. 606; Shorter Edition, p. 365

Wallace combines personal memory and observation, recorded history and scientific research, to give a fascinating account of the beaver and to raise the knotty scientific problem of instinct versus intelligence. In terms of form, the essay might be compared with Diane Ackerman's "Mass Meeting on the Coast" (NR 583), which similarly uses a combination of personal observation and research; in terms of scientific questions, it might be compared with Konrad Z. Lorenz's "The Taming of the Shrew" (NR 588, SE 374) or Alexander Petrunkevitch's "The Spider and the Wasp" (NR 601, SE 387), which probe the issue of animal intelligence.

Wallace's writing raises important rhetorical and intellectual issues. For example, why does Wallace begin with a personal memory? Where else does he use memory or his own observation? Why are these personal moments rhetorically important? Similarly, Wallace incorporates historical accounts that describe beaver behavior. How do such accounts allow him to raise questions about anthropomorphism (attributing human characteristics or motives to animals) and about intelligence (what it means to think)? From a discussion of such questions, you might encourage students to see that rhetorical choices (the well-chosen personal anecdote or example from history) allow writers like Wallace to introduce key intellectual issues.

Analytical Considerations

1. What is the function of personal memory in Wallace's essay? How is it important to theme, style, and persona?
2. Natural history writing often includes a segment of history about the animal under consideration. Where does Wallace incorporate this history? Why?
3. If your library has a good natural history collection, ask your students to check the books by Arthur Dugmore and Enos Mills that Wallace cites (paragraph 5). How has Wallace used his sources? Why does he use his words rather than theirs?
4. What evidence does Wallace give that beavers think? What evidence supports the opposing case for instinct? Has Wallace argued his case successfully?

5. Ask students to analyze Wallace's transitions, particularly the difference between early transitions (which tend to be verbal or narrative) and later ones (which make logical connectives). Why does the mode change during the course of the essay?
6. Explore the ways in which Wallace's conclusion both concludes his argument and opens up new ideas.

Suggested Writing Assignments

1. Write about an animal with which you have had some personal contact; in addition to your own experience, incorporate the views or written accounts of others.
2. Why do human beings anthropomorphize animals? Think about Captain Jonathan Carver's account of beavers (paragraph 3) or another account of animal behavior that similarly attributes human characteristics to animals, and speculate on this human tendency.
3. What does it mean to think? Drawing on the essays of Wallace, Lorenz, and/or Petrunkevitch, write an essay in which you define and illustrate "instinctive behavior" versus "thinking."

Additional questions on this essay will be found in the text (NR 612, SE 371).

ALDO LEOPOLD

Thinking Like a Mountain

The Norton Reader, p. 628 Shorter Edition, p. 372

Leopold's *A Sand County Almanac,* from which this selection comes, is a now-classic work of American nature writing. Leopold (1886–1948) was a wildlife ecologist and environmental philosopher, whose training at the Yale School of Forestry led him to professional service in the U.S. Forest Service and ultimately to a professorship of wildlife management at the University of Wisconsin. In "Thinking Like a Mountain," Leopold focuses on a personal experience—his shooting of an old wolf and her cubs—to argue for a central concept in his philosophy: "the land ethic." According to Leopold, human beings have, through the world's great religious thinkers, learned to regard all men as brothers; they must now learn to expand the notion of community "to include soils, waters, plants, and animals, or collectively the land."

Leopold's essay—actually a journal entry— might provide a good occasion for your class to explore the uses of personal narrative versus more "objective," scientific modes of presenting facts. Leopold here chooses to recount a personal anecdote, which functions almost as a conversion experience, to convey what he learned through years of professional work in the Forest Service. In fact, he might have chosen a more scientific mode of presentation—as he did in other writing. Early in his career, Leopold had believed that valued game species (like deer) could be protected only by killing off their predators (like wolves, bears, and mountain lions). But the history of Arizona's Kaibab Plateau, where the deer herd expanded enormously in the 1920s only to die off from starvation, taught Leopold a different lesson: that man's intervention in nature disrupts the ecosystem and that such intervention can have tragic consequences.

Analytical Considerations

1. Why does Leopold begin by describing—and personifying—nature?
2. Discuss the advantages of personal narration in this essay, perhaps by comparing it with the statements Leopold makes in his textbook, *Game Management* (1933). Or ask your students to contrast the personal mode of Leopold's essay with the different mode of presentation in Joseph Wood Krutch's "The Most Dangerous Predator" (NR 630), which concerns the ecosystems of gulls and terns on Rasa Island and the plight of elephant seals in Baja California. What are the reasons for using personal experience in nature writing? Why might a writer choose not to use the "I"?
3. Leopold uses his own killing of a wolf as an example of human interference in nature. What are the consequences of such acts?
4. Draw out the implications of the title, "Thinking Like a Mountain."

Suggested Writing Assignments

1. At the center of "Thinking Like a Mountain" is Leopold's account of his senseless killing of a wolf. Write about an experience of your own that led you to change your perceptions of—or behavior within—the natural world.
2. Write an essay about something you have observed in nature that has taught you about the interdependence of human beings and their environment.
3. Through library research and/or interviews with scientists or

environmentalists, find out about the destruction of a single plant or animal that has changed the balance of nature. Ideally, do your research on a species of local interest that has relevance to the area in which you live.

KONRAD Z. LORENZ

The Taming of the Shrew

The Norton Reader, p. 588; Shorter Edition, p. 374

Konrad Z. Lorenz recounts his experiments with the water shrew not for scientific colleagues concerned with insectivores, but for the general reader interested in animal behavior. Thus Lorenz presents his findings as a narrative of his discovery of the water shrews and his attempts to keep them alive, rather than as a scientific report of his experiments. While the essay does present new scientific facts and observations, Lorenz largely avoids jargon and elaborates or illustrates his observations to make them comprehensible to the general reader. Most significant in attracting readers is Lorenz's tone. His diction, his use of dialogue, and his admissions of personal dilemma reflect his excitement about his subject and give the reader a sense of the man behind the scientific study.

Analytical Considerations

1. Does Lorenz's approach to scientific observation and experimentation seem classical or innovative, deductive or inductive? What relative weight or emphasis does he give to observation, self-criticism, speculation, and synthesis?
2. Lorenz draws some of his conclusions and records some of his observations of water shrews in terms of analogy with other animals. How is his use of analogy helpful to the general reader? How is it helpful to the scientist?
3. How does Lorenz convey the *process* of scientific discovery in his essay? Detail the steps of the discovery process as Lorenz arranges them.
4. What is the relevance of the epigraph for the essay? When Lorenz describes the behavior of the shrews when offered "a large edible frog" (paragraph 19), what philosophical commentary does he offer?

5. Students are likely to accept Lorenz as an authority and trust his observations and conclusions. To what extent is Lorenz's authority dependent on his use of factual evidence? To what extent is it dependent on his ability to engage the reader's interest and sympathy personally? Discuss the role of persona in creating authority.

Suggested Writing Assignments

1. Rewrite Lorenz's report as a simple summary of his experiments and findings. To which essay in the "Science" section is this summary most similar in tone? How does your summary differ from most writing in the "Nature" section?
2. Write an essay in response to this question raised by Lorenz: "But man should abstain from judging his innocently-cruel fellow creatures, for even if nature sometimes 'shrieks against his creed,' what pain does he himself not inflict upon the living creatures that he hunts for pleasure and not for food?" (paragraph 19).

Additional questions on this essay will be found in the text (NR 600–601, SE 386–87).

ALEXANDER PETRUNKEVITCH

The Spider and the Wasp

The Norton Reader, p. 601; Shorter Edition, p. 387

Two fascinating, if repellent, creatures allow Petrunkevitch to discuss animal instinct versus intelligence, the same issue that excites Carl Sagan, Konrad Z. Lorenz, and David Rains Wallace. The structure of Petrunkevitch's essay differs, however, from that of these other writers. Whereas Lorenz *narrates the process* of his discovery of and experimentation with water shrews and Sagan *mounts a formal argument* using chimpanzees and other primates to illustrate his points, "The Spider and the Wasp" begins with a detailed description of the physiological makeup of the tarantula, continues with an account of what happens when it encounters the digger wasp of the genus *Pepsis*, and concludes with deductions about animal reasoning versus instinctive behavior. You might discuss these different organizations that writers choose, suggesting that students, too, should consider a range of options in their own work.

Analytical Considerations

1. Ask students to describe Petrunkevitch's opening paragraph, perhaps comparing it with others in this section. What advantages do they see in his straightforward, workmanlike statement of purpose?
2. Plot the organization of this essay. Where do descriptive paragraphs tend to occur? argumentative paragraphs? Why?
3. What details about the tarantula or the digger wasp were the most fascinating? How does Petrunkevitch's style contribute to the effect?
4. Is there any evidence that tarantulas behave intelligently? How does Petrunkevitch treat possible evidence against his case?

Suggested Writing Assignments

1. Write an essay about the spider or the wasp, using facts from Petrunkevitch's article but incorporating more information on human responses to the animal (whether personal, historical, or mythological). In other words, write an essay closer in form to that by Wallace on the beaver (NR 606, SE 365) or Diane Ackerman on the monarch butterfly (NR 583).
2. Rewrite some of the material from Lorenz's "The Taming of the Shrew" (NR 588, SE 374) or Sagan's "The Abstractions of Beasts" (NR 613, SE 392) so that it follows the form of Petrunkevitch's essay: description of the animal, narration of its behavior in a specific situation, conclusions about its "instinctive" or "reasoning" ability.

Additional questions on this essay will be found in the text (NR 605, SE 391)

CARL SAGAN

The Abstractions of Beasts

The Norton Reader, p. 613; Shorter Edition, p. 392

A professor of astronomy and space science, Carl Sagan has earned a reputation as a controversial and imaginative thinker whose ideas challenge the anthropocentrism underlying traditional scientific and philosophical thought. Sagan is perhaps best known as a scientist with solid academic credentials who publicly airs his belief in extraterrestrial life. In this essay, taken from *The Dragons of Eden*, Sagan argues that the distinction humans rely on to set themselves apart from and above other animals—the ability to reason and imagine—is false. He bases his assertion on evidence that at least some beasts, notably primates, seem to have abstracting powers. Although less extensive than in humans, primates' ability to "reason" demands that we reevaluate ourselves and our ethical views. Perhaps threatening, certainly controversial, Sagan's essay is lively and forceful in its skillful interweaving of theory, anecdote, and illustration.

Analytical Considerations

1. Who said of animals, "The defect that hinders communication betwixt them and us, why may it not be on our part as well as theirs" (paragraph 2)? Why does Sagan quote this philosopher early in his essay?
2. Consider spending some class time on a careful analysis of the introduction. Is there a thesis statement? Does it predict the scope of the essay?
3. Analyze the ways in which Sagan develops his argument, letting students point out the two distinct parts (one includes paragraphs 3 to 14; two includes paragraphs 15 to 26).
4. Ask students about Sagan's tone. Is he belligerent or provocative? For reasons of conviction or rhetoric?
5. Ask what paragraphs constitute the conclusion. Is it expected? Effective?
6. This is a good essay to teach the technique of the rhetorical question. Ask students to note where they occur (paragraphs 1, 2, 5, 14, 23, 25, and 26) and how they function.
7. Although this essay is included in the "Nature" section, some readers might feel that it represents "scientific reporting" rather than "nature writing." Ask students to analyze the essay according to Robert Finch's definition in "Being at Two with Nature" (NR 567, SE 349) Does it fit Finch's definition? Alternatively, compare it with David Rains Wallace's "The Mind of the Beaver" (NR 606, SE 365) and discuss the differences between the two writer's approaches to animals.

Suggested Writing Assignments

1. Two abilities—abstract thinking and language use—seem to be the most important factors in intelligence. Define *abstraction* and *language*, and explain their relationship to each other. Why do these elements seem crucial in a consideration of the value of species?
2. Write an essay in response to either of Sagan's questions (paragraph 23):
   a. "How smart does a chimpanzee have to be before killing constitutes murder?"
   b. "If chimpanzees have consciousness, if they are capable of abstractions, do they not have what until now has been described as 'human rights'?"

CHIEF SEATTLE

Letter to President Pierce

The Norton Reader, p. 626; Shorter Edition, p. 399

Chief Seattle's "Letter to President Pierce," like the essays by Aldo Leopold (NR 628, SE 372) and Joseph Wood Krutch (NR 630) that are included in the "Nature" section, argues for the interdependence of man and the natural world—in Seattle's words, "All things are connected." Yet these three writers argue their cases in quite different ways, using different styles and rhetorical strategies. Seattle's "Letter," for example, abounds in maxims: "Continue to contaminate your bed, and you will one night suffocate in your own waste" (paragraph 5) or "Whatever befalls the earth befalls the sons of earth" (paragraph 3). Krutch's article, in contrast, draws heavily on scientific and historical data; indeed, his term for interdependence comes from modern science: *cybernetics,* a "self-regulating mechanism." Leopold's journal entry uses a past personal experience—his killing of a wolf—to show the limitations of man's perspective and to encourage more global thinking about the natural world. You might discuss with students the advantages of each strategy, why a writer might adopt one rather than another, and how they might try similar strategies in their own writing.

You might also use Seattle's "Letter," and other essays in the "Nature" section, to discuss how a writer gains authority to speak out on an issue of public importance. Today, we might assume that Seattle, chief of the Dwamish, Suquamish, and allied Indian tribes, would be respected for the wisdom about the natural world he and his people had accumulated but writing in 1855, Seattle knew that many Americans considered the Indian to be only "a savage." Seattle takes this common view and recasts it ironically—repeating the phrase "the red man is a savage and does not understand" at moments when the white man's behavior seems most foolish and destructive.

Analytical Considerations

1. Listeners who heard Chief Seattle speak said that he was an impressive public orator. What elements of his style would contribute to this effect?
2. Ask students to compare and contrast Chief Seattle's ironic style with Leopold's more meditative, almost religious language—or with Terry Tempest Williams' (NR 639, SE 401) attempt to blend traditions of feminine, western American, and Indian rhetoric.

Suggested Writing Assignments

1. Choose a maxim from Chief Seattle's "Letter" as the thesis for an argument you wish to make about a topic of environmental importance. Examples: "Continue to contaminate your bed, and you will one night suffocate in your own waste (paragraph 5) or "All things share the same breath—the beasts, the trees, the man" (paragraph 2).
2. Write a letter to the president of the United States on an environmental issue of relevance today or recast the material from another essay in this section into the form of a letter to the president.
3. In many essays on environmental topics, a member of a minority group (or a person holding a minority opinion) must persuade the majority to alter its course. Write an argument on an environmental topic that concerns you deeply, using your position as a minority writer as part of your strategy for persuading the majority to change its view.

Additional questions on this essay will be found in the text (NR 627–28, SE 400–01).

TERRY TEMPEST WILLIAMS

The Clan of One-Breasted Women

The Norton Reader, p. 639; Shorter Edition, p. 401

Williams explains the literal meaning of her title in the first paragraph: The women in her family suffer from breast cancer and the mastectomies that frequently result. Students may also want to know about the mythological tribe of women warriors, the Amazons, who according to some legends cut off their right breasts in order to wield their bows and arrows more freely. This allusion prepares for Williams' discussion, later in the essay, of her dilemma about whether or not she, as a Mormon woman, should fight governmental authorities and risk imprisonment. Should she, like other Mormons, accept passively the cancer that threatens her, or should she, like the Amazons, fight actively against it?

Williams is naturalist-in-residence at the Utah Museum of Natural History and the author of two books of nature writing: *Pieces of White Shell: A Journey to Navajo Land* (1984) and *Coyote's Canyon* (1989). This essay combines powerful personal experiences with research into historical and environmental issues to argue against nuclear testing in the desert. Students may find the combination of personal experience and research data rhetorically useful if they choose to write essays that take a stand on environmental issues. You might suggest that they use Williams' essay as a model for structure and for argument.

Analytical Considerations

1. The first section of Williams' essay narrates family history and personal memory. How does Williams shape her narration to build to a startling revelation?
2. How—and why—does a writer incorporate factual evidence into what is essentially a personal essay? In the second section (paragraphs 20 to 29), Williams condenses facts from several historical and governmental studies (see accompanying footnotes). You might ask students to look up these sources and explain how Williams uses evidence from her research, especially the quoted phrases. You might also discuss with them why Williams does *not* quote her research materials in some places, whether because she can assume knowledge on the part of her readers or because her personal rendition of the materials is more compelling.

3. What influence does Mormon culture and religion have on Williams' personal behavior? How does she convey her attitude toward her religious background, especially in the third section?

4. Williams' rhetorical strategies include many that might be called "feminist": naming her mother and grandmothers, recounting her "dream" and the song of the Shoshoni women, metaphorically comparing the pangs of women giving birth with the death pangs of the desert, referring to her memory of the Joshua trees, and more generally, as in her title, alluding to women's history and myth. Instructors interested in the possibilities of feminist rhetoric might want to consider the use of women's history and myth as an alternative to more traditionally "masculine" modes of argument in pieces of environmental writing like Abbey's or Leopold's.

Suggested Writing Assignments

1. Choose an environmental issue for which you have personal experience and factual data to draw on. (If you don't have factual data when you start, do research to collect the relevant evidence.) Write an essay about that issue in which you, like Williams, combine personal experience and objective facts.

2. Use an incident or story in your family's history as the starting point for an essay that makes an argument (explicit or implicit) about some important public issue.

3. Consult one of the sources Williams cites in her footnotes to learn more about nuclear testing in Utah and other western states. Instead of a personal essay, write a historical summary of the events that lie behind Williams' family experience. What purpose might your version of the events have that Williams' does not?

ETHICS

GARY SOTO

The Pie

The Norton Reader, p. 647; Shorter Edition, p. 409

Gary Soto teaches English and Chicano Studies at the University of California, Berkeley; he is a poet and short-story writer as well as an essayist. "The Pie" was published in *A Summer Life* (1990), a collection of essays about his childhood in a Chicano community in Fresno, California: "what I knew best was at ground-level," Soto writes. In this "ground level" essay he creates the physical and moral world of a six-year-old.

"The Pie" is a severely focused account of personal experience. Accounts in the "Personal Report" section that focus on a single experience provide useful contrasts to Soto's: Maya Angelou's "Graduation" (NR 19, SE 11), for example, in which she describes the events leading up to her graduation as well as the ceremony itself, or Bruno Bettelheim's "A Victim" (NR 29, SE 21), in which he describes the routines of life in a concentration camp and the consequences of his visit to an infirmary within it. Students should notice how abruptly Soto begins and ends his account and how, unlike Angelou and Bettelheim, he virtually eliminates preliminary and contextual information.

In addition to his focus on personal experience, Soto makes his moral generalizations those of a six-year-old. Other essays in *The Norton Reader* provide useful contrasts: for example, Gloria Naylor's "Mommy, What Does 'Nigger' Mean?" (NR 378, SE 227), in which she frames a childhood experience with general statements clearly those of her adult self. Soto's general statements are the personal and unqualified ones of a child. They are nevertheless moral generalizations: "The Pie" is appropriately included among the essays in "Ethics."

Analytical Considerations

1. Although Soto virtually eliminates preliminary and contextual information from his account of stealing a pie, he does suggest some. You might, as an exercise in inference, ask students to look at this statement (in paragraph 4): "I knew an apple got Eve into

deep trouble with snakes because Sister Marie had shown us a film about Adam and Eve being cast into the desert." If the exercise is profitable, have them locate other statements that suggest other inferences about the child's past and his milieu.

2. Look at the first sentence of "The Pie" as an example of a child's personal and unqualified moral generalization. Ask students to find similar generalizations and try recasting one or more of them as adult generalizations.

3. Although Soto focuses "The Pie" on the experience of a six-year-old, he uses the resources of his adult and unusually expressive language to create it. Try looking at a sentence like "Once, at the German Market, I stood before a rack of pies, my sweet tooth gleaming and the juice of guilt wetting my underarms" (paragraph 2). Have students consider the expressive elements of Soto's language and find other sentences whose vivid language pleases them.

Suggested Writing Assignments

1. Follow Soto in describing an ethical dilemma you experienced as a child. Try to restrict yourself to the perspective of a child as severely as he does.

2. Rewrite your first essay *or* write another essay about an ethical dilemma you experienced as a child in which you (re)cast your moral generalizations in the "impersonal" and analytic language of an adult.

Samuel L. Clemens

Advice to Youth

The Norton Reader, p. 662; Shorter Edition, p. 411

Samuel L. Clemens—or Mark Twain—is probably nineteenth-century America's best comic author and satirist. "Advice to Youth," a lecture Clemens gave in 1882, was not published until 1923; we do not know the circumstances under which he gave it. In it he mimics a conventional script, precepts for behavior delivered by age to youth. Undoubtedly his audience expected comedy. Nevertheless, he begins seriously and can be taken ironically—that is, as saying one thing and meaning another—from the beginning only if his reputation for comedy precedes him. His first precept, "Always obey your parents" (paragraph 2) mimics seriousness; he tips us off to its irony when he qualifies it with "when they are present." This pattern of precept subverted by comedy persists throughout the lecture, and students should be able to identify Clemens' two modes: the ironic and the comic.

Most of the adults who came to hear Clemens would have expected to be amused, and undoubtedly many of them were, even though he satirizes the pompous advice that age delivers to youth. Irony is, however, an unstable mode whose success presupposes ideal auditors and readers. Ironists contribute to its success by evoking them. But it can go wrong. Can students imagine a range of responses from Clemens' audience, from enjoyment to indignation?

Satire is for as well as against, but we can identify what Clemens is satirizing more surely than we can identify what he is commending. Students who have read Jonathan Swift's "A Modest Proposal" (NR 878, SE 522) might look again at paragraphs 29 and 30, where Swift lists "other expedients," that is, what he is for. Is it possible to make a similar list of what Clemens is for?

Analytical Considerations

1. You might make sure students recognize irony by having them underline Clemens' precepts and mark the places where he modulates from irony to comedy.
2. Ask students to consider what qualities an ideal auditor or reader of Clemens' lecture would possess and how Clemens might be seen as trying to evoke them.
3. What is Clemens for? Ask students, individually or in groups, to list or describe the values implicit in his lecture.

Suggested Writing Assignments

1. Take Polonius's precept-filled speech to his son Laertes (*Hamlet* 1.3) and use it as the skeleton of a talk in which you alternate irony and comedy in the manner of Clemens.
2. Invent a series of precepts for youth to deliver to age and use it as the skeleton of a talk in which you alternate irony and comedy in the manner of Clemens.
3. Imagine yourself an auditor offended by Clemens' talk and write a letter to its sponsors berating them for inviting him to give it. Or imagine yourself an adult amused by Clemens' talk and write a

letter to its sponsors commending them for inviting him to give it. Or write both letters.
4. Write a letter of advice to an adult about to give a high school commencement address as to what kind of advice to give and how to give it without becoming vulnerable to satire.

Additional questions on this essay will be found in the text (NR 675, SE 414).

Willard Gaylin

What You See Is the Real You

The Norton Reader, p. 675; Shorter Edition, p. 414

Willard Gaylin announces as his intention rectifying an error promulgated by psychoanalysis that the inner self is real, the outer self "an illusion or pretender" (paragraph 2). At the beginning of the same paragraph he gains authority by identifying himself as a psychoanalyst. He has two connected purposes: to deny the existence of an inner self and to show how the concept of an inner self muddies moral judgments. You might ask students to locate instances where he connects, explicitly and implicitly, his two purposes.

This essay was published in the *New York Times* in 1977. Gaylin's audience is general, and he addresses them directly, using imperatives and speaking to them as *you*. He also writes rather short, simply constructed sentences organized in brief paragraphs. The essay hovers between argument, deliberately simplified argument, and advice. Gaylin makes it clear where he stands, so that his argument commands attention. In making moral judgments, behavior rather than the intentions of an inner self is what counts.

Analytical Considerations

1. Gaylin illustrates two kinds of moral confusion emerging from the concept of an inner self: that persons with good inner selves can behave badly and that persons with less than good inner selves can behave well. You might ask students to locate examples of each in his essay.
2. Ask students to underline Gaylin's imperatives and *you*'s to see how these forms of direct address convert argument to advice. While

these forms are appropriate to Gaylin's purposes, students often use them inappropriately in description and exposition. This exercise should call attention to their effect.

3. Gaylin speaks of the inner *man* and the outer *man* and uses *man* as a generic. Suggest to students that they use inner *self* and outer *self* (as above) and refer them to "'Generic' *He*" (G p. 66) for other substitutions. Have them make and then discuss their substitutions.

Suggested Writing Assignments

1. Write an essay in which you either argue against Gaylin's assertion "You are for the most part what you seem to be, not what you would wish to be, nor, indeed, what you believe yourself to be" (paragraph 8) or pick up on his qualification "for the most part" and modify his assertion.

2. Write an essay in which you describe your inner self. In addition, consider instances in which the concept of an inner self is useful to you, dangerous, or both.

Additional questions on this essay will be found in the text (NR 676–77, SE 415–16).

MARY MIDGLEY

Trying Out One's New Sword

The Norton Reader, p. 665; Shorter Edition, p. 416

Mary Midgley is a British philosopher who writes chiefly on ethics. This essay comes from a volume called *Heart and Mind: The Varieties of Moral Experience;* another volume of hers bears the arresting title *Wickedness: A Philosophical Essay.* She has also written on animal rights and women's rights. She often poses ethical questions through a hypothetical situation, sometimes invented, sometimes real, as in this essay, when the Japanese samurai finds a traveler on whom to try out his new sword.

"Trying Out One's New Sword" should encourage students to consider their own criteria for making moral judgments. William H. Perry, Jr. (*Forms of Intellectual and Ethical Development in the College Years*) charts this development as a progress from imposing strict categories of right and wrong to accepting multiple perspectives to analyzing and evaluating multiple perspectives. These stages roughly correspond to what Midgley calls *"crude* opinions" or "slapdash yes-or-no matter[s]," "moral isolationism" or "real moral scepticism," and the "hard work" of "asking the questions which arise *from where we stand,* questions which we can see the sense of."

The moral judgments that preoccupy students are likely to be those between, say, youth and adult cultures rather than those between Western and other cultures that Midgley describes. It is nevertheless possible for them to move from her judgments to their own when they understand her model for making them. Moral isolationism, as Midgley puts it, "would lay down a general ban on moral reasoning." She then turns around to suggest that when we adopt moral isolationism, we do so because we disapprove of "human hypocrisy and other forms of wickedness," and that this disapproval is itself a moral judgment.

Analytical Considerations

1. Before assigning Midgley's essay, you might describe to students the custom of trying out one's new sword and ask them to record their reactions. After they have read Midgley's essay, you might also ask them to describe and analyze their reactions using her analytic categories: *"crude* opinions," "moral isolationism," and the "hard work" of "asking the questions which arise *from where we stand,* questions which we can see the sense of."
2. In the dialogue between Midgley the condemner of the Samurai custom of trying out one's new sword and Midgley as a defender of it (paragraph 11), the values at issue between them are discipline and devotion, the value of life, and consent. Ask students to discuss which criteria they value, which not, and why, and which Midgley values. They should also notice how she ironizes both Samurai values not generally accepted in Western culture and Western values projected onto Samurai culture.
3. You might ask students to supply their own instances of crude and hypocritical judgments. If they supply chiefly the judgments of others directed against themselves, challenge them to supply counterexamples of their own crude and hypocritical judgments. If you do, be prepared to supply a couple of your own.

Suggested Writing Assignments

1. Moral isolationism blocks praise as well as blame, both with respect to other cultures and our own. Choose two aspects of a non-Western culture, one that you will praise and one that you will blame, and write an essay in which you do so with recourse to the kind of complex model for making judgments that Midgley advocates. Use your own anthropology text or an anthropology text used at your institution.

2. Choose two aspects of American culture—one for praise and one for blame—and write an essay in which you praise one and blame another.

3. Take a decision you have made with respect to your own behavior (for example, concerning sex, drinking, drugs, money, honesty) and describe how you made it. Then write a letter in which you explain your decision to someone who has made a different decision concerning a similar problem.

4. Of the Samurai custom of trying out a new sword Midgley writes "we shall probably find it easier to think calmly about it than we should with a contemporary one, such as female circumcision in Africa or the Chinese Cultural Revolution" (paragraph 3). Do library research on one or the other and write an essay in which you explain, with reference to your findings, how you understand Midgley's statement.

MICHAEL LEVIN

The Case for Torture

The Norton Reader, p. 677; Shorter Edition, p. 421

Michael Levin is a professor of philosophy at the City College, City University of New York. He writes for nonprofessional readers as well as for professional philosophers; this essay originally appeared in the "My Turn" column of *Newsweek*. Levin is calculatedly aware that, making a case for torture, he is making an unpopular, even shocking case: "It is generally assumed that torture is impossible," he begins, "a throwback to a more brutal age." Although he clarifies the circumstances under which torture is permissible, his position that it is justified in extreme and in less extreme cases is controversial. The use of torture by regimes we condemn makes even more shocking his argument that we must, as he puts it, "choose to inflict pain as one way of preserving order" (paragraph 12).

This essay may profitably be read along with Paul Fussell's "Thank God for the Atom Bomb" (NR 711, SE 433). Fussell, like Levin, makes a controversial case. His essay is, of course, longer than Levin's: He lets readers hear the voices of those who disagree with him, even though he denies their counterarguments. Because his essay is more inclusive than Levin's, his case for the bombing of Hiroshima and Nagasaki is neither simple nor clear-cut. The genre of his essay is persuasion: He wants readers to understand his position even if they do not agree with it. Some students, as readers and as writers, prefer persuasive strategies.

Levin makes a case for torture like a debater, and like a debater, he is out to win. He illustrates his argument with hypothetical and clear-cut cases rather than complex and ambiguous ones. For example, he is sure that we have the right terrorist to torture and that the bomb is really there (paragraph 3). He brings up the counterarguments of those who disagree with him—as in a debate, they are his opponents—to rebut them rather than to acknowledge that they make his case less clear cut, more hedged with complexity. His genre is argument: He wants us to agree with his position. Some students, as readers and as writers, prefer argumentative strategies.

Analytical Considerations

1. In paragraph 12 Levin poses as the alternative to "inflict[ing] pain as one way of preserving order" becoming paralyzed "in the face of evil." You might ask students whether this is a fair statement of alternatives? If not, can they produce fairer statements?
2. Have students look at Levin's hypothetical cases. Can they invent hypothetical countercases? Of what sort? What are the advantages and disadvantages of arguing from hypothetical cases?
3. You might use this essay to ask students to consider what constitutes an ethical decision? Can a decision to torture and a decision not to torture both be ethical? What are their criteria for ethical decisions? Are they the same as Mary Midgley's in "Trying Out One's New Sword" (NR 665, SE 416)?
4. You might ask students to consider what leads them to prefer either persuasion or argument, both as writers and as readers. Do they, as writers, self-consciously make choices as to which mode they use? Should they?

Suggested Writing Assignments

1. Write an essay in which you argue against torture with debater's strategies—use hypothetical and clear-cut cases and rebut rather than incorporate counterarguments.
2. Write an essay in which you make a persuasive case either for or against torture, with the aim of having readers understand your position whether or not they agree with it.
3. Read Ursula LeGuin's story "Those Who Walk Away from Omelas"; it appears in her collection *The Wind's Four Quarters* and is frequently anthologized. Write an essay in which you consider how she complicates Levin's position that we must "choose to inflict pain as one way of preserving order"?

Additional questions on this essay will be found in the text (NR 679–80, SE 423).

STEPHEN JAY GOULD

The Terrifying Normalcy of AIDS

The Norton Reader, p. 702; Shorter Edition, p. 424

In this essay, Gould— a biologist, paleontologist, and historian of science—turns his attention to the AIDS "pandemic." Like Gould's regular column in *Natural History* magazine, "The Terrifying Normalcy of AIDS" was written for a lay audience: It appeared in the *New York Times Magazine* in April 1987. Gould characterizes AIDS as both normal and terrifying: He wants us to see it as occupying a middle position between just another disease for which "medicine will soon generate a cure" and "something so irregular that it must have been visited on us to teach us a moral lesson" (paragraph 14).

Gould also wants to describe and criticize a particular American belief, that technology will solve all our problems. This belief he embodies in Walt Disney World's Epcot Center. His essay thus has a double focus: the power of nature (of which AIDS is part) and our false confidence in technological fixes.

Analytic Considerations

1. It is likely that at least some students will have been to Epcot Center. You might ask them, before they read "The Terrifying Normalcy of AIDS," to describe it—in discussion or in writing—so that all students can consider what aspects of American culture it can be made to embody. Students who have not been to Epcot Center may be asked, after a discussion of its uses, to locate in their own experience emblems that can be made to carry equivalent meanings.
2. Gould uses current events, historical information, and scientific data to make his case. You might ask students to identify particular examples of each.
3. Gould divides "The Terrifying Normalcy of Aids" into four sections by means of spacing: paragraphs 1 to 5, 6 to 9, 10 to 13, and 14 to 16. Ask students to consider whether these spatial divisions correspond to units of exposition and argument. You might also ask them, singly or in groups, to make up subtitles for each section.

Suggested Writing Assignments

1. "The Terrifying Normalcy of AIDS" appeared in 1987. Do library research to ascertain and report on the current state of what is known about the prevention and cure of AIDS. Write an essay in which you organize this information to support Gould's two-part assertion, "AIDS works by a *mechanism*—and we can discover it" (paragraph 16), to question it, or both.
2. Write an essay using different illustrative material—that is, something other than AIDS—either to support Gould's assertion that "The message of Orlando—the inevitability of technological solutions—is wrong, and we need to understand why" (paragraph 10), to question it, or both.
3. Read Susan Sontag's *AIDS and Its Metaphors* and, using her analysis, write an essay in which you expand Gould's statement that AIDS causes some people to "panic in confusion and seek a scapegoat for something so irregular that it must have been visited upon us to teach us a moral lesson" (paragraph 14).

KILDARE DOBBS

The Shatterer of Worlds

The Norton Reader, p. 705; Shorter Edition, p. 427

"The Shatterer of Worlds" is a "you-are-there" essay in which Dobbs, a Canadian journalist, narrates the story of a Japanese girl, Emiko, who was in Hiroshima on August 5, 1945, the day an American B-29 bomber dropped the first atomic bomb. Dobbs periodically interrupts Emiko's story to narrate, briefly, the actions and responses of the American crew of the *Enola Gay*, the B-29 that dropped the bomb. Some students will undoubtedly have read John Hersey's *Hiroshima* or other accounts of the bombing; for others, Dobbs' narrative will be the first. It might be instructive to ask open questions about it to engage as wide a range of responses as possible. What kind of responses do students think Dobbs is looking for and why do they think so? Does he elicit these responses from them?

Dobbs' alternating stories do more than provide two different perspectives on the same event: They juxtapose the physical and emotional pain of Emiko, her family, and other residents of Hiroshima with the detachment of the American crew. Dobbs' technique of juxtaposition—or, in film, crosscutting—is designed powerfully to contrast the suffering and helpless victims with their unconcerned and amoral destroyers. Then, at the end of his essay (paragraphs 39 to 41), he turns from stories to comment —but not, students should notice, to comment *on* the stories. That he reserves for the last paragraph, in which Emiko's scar becomes a "tiny metaphor" and "a faint but eloquent reminder of the scar on humanity's conscience." This metaphor evokes the moral judgments that have remained implicit rather than explicit throughout the essay.

Analytical Considerations

1. You-are-there narrative precludes footnotes; it aims to make readers think they are there. Dobbs was not. Where, other than from Emiko, do students think Dobbs got his information? Could she have supplied all the Japanese details concerning the bombing of Hiroshima? Is Dobbs' you-are-there presentation more or less convincing than a presentation that documents sources and makes visible the assembling of details?
2. You might ask students to notice Dobbs' rather short, simply

constructed sentences organized in brief and even in one-sentence paragraphs. Look at some of the latter and consider their effect. Why are they more appropriate to narrative than to argument?

Suggested Writing Assignments

1. Take an account of a contemporary or historical event in which sources are documented and the author's putting details together is visible and turn it into a you-are-there narrative. Then note, briefly, what you have added and what you have suppressed. Students might be asked to share sources, their own narratives, and their comments in small groups.
2. Read Paul Fussell's "Thank God for the Atom Bomb" (NR 711, SE 433) and use information he supplies either to revise Dobbs' juxtaposed narratives by keeping one (either Japanese or American) and writing a substitute for the other or, alternatively, to write substitutes for both. Decide before you begin what moral weight you want to assign to each narrative.

PAUL FUSSELL

Thank God for the Atom Bomb

The Norton Reader, p. 711; Shorter Edition, p. 433

"Thank God for the Atom Bomb" was originally published in *The New Republic* in August 1981. It became the title essay in Fussell's *Thank God for the Atom Bomb and Other Essays,* published in 1988, forty-three years after the bombings of Hiroshima and Nagasaki; he speaks of writing on their forty-second anniversary, prompted, he says, "by the long debate about the ethics, if any, of that ghastly affair." Fussell takes on a number of the debaters, mostly those questioning the necessity and the morality of the bombings. Students might be asked to compile a bibliography from his essay: They will find names, sometimes the titles of books and periodicals, never dates. Those who want to use Fussell's essay as an introduction to the debate, not to mention those who want to check Fussell's use of sources, will have to search further. This exercise might lead to a discussion of acknowledging sources and the advantages and disadvantages of scholarly and popular conventions with respect to annotation.

You will want students to look at Fussell's persuasive strategies, notably his use of autobiographical material and the way he begins with a long discussion concerning the value of experience. He argues *ad hominem* (that is, *to the man*) two ways: in making his own case and in arguing against the cases of others. You might have students identify his *ad hominem* arguments against others and, in particular, look at what he says about the "offensive implications" of using them against John Kenneth Galbraith and Michael Sherry (paragraphs 8 and 9).

Fussell's essay may profitably discussed along with two other essays in the "Ethics" section, Michael Levin's "The Case for Torture" (NR 677, SE 421) and Kildare Dobbs' "The Shatterer of Worlds" (NR 705, SE 427). Both Levin and Fussell deal with controversial cases and acknowledge the fact. Having students reread Levin's essay may heighten their awareness of his detachment and Fussell's engagement. Both Dobbs and Fussell deal with similar material and include the experience of others. Having students reread Dobbs' essay may heighten their awareness of how Dobbs assimilates Emiko's experience while Fussell borrows and makes visible his borrowing of the experience of a variety of other persons.

Analytic Considerations

1. You might focus a discussion of Fussell's use of sources by having students locate and read the debate between Joseph Alsop and David Joravsky in the *New York Review of Books* (or bring copies of it to class). This debate, "reduced to a collision between experience and theory, was conducted with a certain civilized respect for evidence," according to Fussell (paragraphs 14 to 16). Does Fussell fairly summarize and characterize the debate?
2. Have students look at the various *ad hominem* arguments Fussell employs. Could he argue in ways other than *ad hominem*? How? What are the advantages and disadvantages of *ad hominem* arguments?

Suggested Writing Assignments

1. Write an essay in which you argue for a position that personally involves you. Rather than disguising your involvement and adopting a detached stance, feature it; use it to gain authority over your subject.

2. Write an essay in which you argue for a position that does not personally involve you. Use someone else's experience. Either make visible your putting together details of that experience in the manner of Fussell or write a you-are-there account in the manner of Dobbs.
3. Rewrite Fussell's essay using the argumentative strategies of Levin in "The Case for Torture."
4. Fussell concludes his essay: "The past, which as always did not know the future, acted in ways that ask to be imagined before they are condemned. Or even simplified." Write an essay in which you discuss "Thank God for the Atom Bomb" in light of Fussell's own criteria for moral judgment.

Additional questions on this essay will be found in the text (NR 724, SE 446).

HISTORY

HENRY DAVID THOREAU

The Battle of the Ants

The Norton Reader, p. 741; Shorter Edition, p. 447

Taken from the chapter in *Walden* titled "Brute Neighbors," "The Battle of the Ants" is not so much history as natural history. Yet, because Thoreau alludes to historical battles and imitates the conventions of history writing, this brief account provides an opportunity for discussing what constitutes a historical "event" and how a historical style of writing gives status to some events (and not others). The battle Thoreau describes would not normally be considered "historical": It is, after all, only a struggle between two species of insect. But Thoreau's account leads us to ponder whether human struggles—which we call wars—should be considered historical either. Wars are given the greatest attention by historians—their maneuvers recorded in detail, their leaders and soldiers praised, their outcomes treated as decisive in human lives—and Thoreau leads us to ask whether this approach to history should be our model.

Analytical Considerations

1. In the long first paragraph, Thoreau alludes to two well-known wars: the battles recorded in Homer's *Iliad* and the American Revolution, particularly the battle of Lexington and Concord (where "the shot heard 'round the world" was fired). What effect does Thoreau intend? By comparing the battle of the ants to classical Greek and American wars, he writes a form of "mock heroic," which both elevates the actions of the ants and paradoxically deflates the warlike actions of men.

2. Why does Thoreau describe the wounds of the ants in such detail? You might think of his description as an example of natural history as well as an imitation of historical writing.

3. In the final paragraph, Thoreau alludes to American and European entomologists, also called natural historians. Thoreau's style in this paragraph, however, is not that of a scientist but a parody of the historian's. Why?

4. What significance might there be in the fact that Thoreau dates the

battle of his ants "five years before the passage of Webster's Fugitive—Slave Bill" (paragraph 3)? In Thoreau's mind, what kind of historical event seems to be genuinely significant?

Suggested Writing Assignments

1. Read an account of the battle of Lexington and Concord (where Thoreau lived); then analyze the section of Thoreau's account that alludes to this battle, suggesting how Thoreau's fellow citizens might have responded to his allusions.
2. Look up a description of the behavior of ants in a book by one of the entomologists Thoreau refers to or in another scientific textbook. Compare and contrast the style of the scientist with Thoreau's. What different effects are intended?

Additional questions on this essay will be found in the text (NR 743–44, SE 449–450).

JOHN LIVINGSTON LOWES

Time in the Middle Ages

The Norton Reader, p. 749; Shorter Edition, p. 450

What was it like to live during the Middle Ages? That question engages John Livingston Lowes as he describes the system of time used by Chaucer and his contemporaries. To help students imagine themselves back into another era, you might ask them first to enumerate the ways in which they order their lives according to mechanical time—by means of clocks, watches, digital mechanisms embedded in cars, computers, microwave ovens, and the like. You might also ask them to try functioning without these mechanisms for a day, perhaps operating according to the medieval system of "inequal hours." Whether or not you attempt these experiential approaches, Lowes' essay can help students think about the different ways in which history would have been recorded in the fourteenth century versus the way it is recorded in the twentieth.

Analytical Considerations

1. Ask students to chart on the blackboard the means by which the days of the week were determined. Then ask how languages other than

English and French have retained traces of this system.

2. If you have students who come from non-European countries, you might ask if they can contribute a time scheme different from the one Lowes describes or the one we operate with today. This question may reveal how time schemes reflect cultural differences, but it may also turn out that mechanical time has overtaken the world.

3. Why does Lowes present his material as he does—from the order of the planets, to the system of hours, to the days of the week, to the astrological signs? Could he have used a different order?

4. Bring in a copy of the astrological chart Lowes refers to in the final paragraph. (It appears in many modern books on astrology.) Why do we continue to pursue aspects of this old time system in the modern day? What human need or desire does it serve?

Suggested Writing Assignments

1. Have you ever experienced a portion of your life outside the normal, mechanical system of time? If so, write an essay about your experience, perhaps comparing it with the routine of ordinary life.

2. Study a modern reproduction of the chart Lowes refers to in the final paragraph, and speculate why this older approach to time still appeals to humans in the modern world.

Additional questions on this essay will be found in the text (NR 753–54, SE 455).

BARBARA TUCHMAN

"This Is the End of the World": The Black Death

The Norton Reader, p. 754; Shorter Edition, p. 455

Barbara Tuchman's account of the Black Death, from her book *A Distant Mirror: The Calamitous Fourteenth Century*, is a brilliant, justly famous recreation of a famous historical event. Tuchman describes the movement of the disease from central Asia through Europe; creates statistical data to convey its enormous impact on European society; records human responses to the plague, from the horribly selfish to the literally saintly; and explores various medieval explanations for the cause and meaning of the plague. For many students, this essay will represent the classic—and best—example of historical writing in this section, for Tuchman is a master of the conventions and a skilled practitioner.

Analytical Considerations

1. For many students, Tuchman's "'This Is the End of the World'" will seem much more like "history" than other selections in this unit. Why? What features of her writing signal that this is history?
2. At some point, perhaps initially, perhaps *in medias res,* ask students what facts about the Black Death they remember best. Then consider why they remember these facts, what techniques in Tuchman's rendering make them memorable.
3. Tuchman's chapter begins with a date (October 1347) and initially proceeds in chronological order. At what point does chronology cease to organize the chapter? What other organization supplants it?
4. Ask students to summarize what each section of the essay does and how Tuchman moves from section to section.
5. In the final two sections (beginning with paragraphs 26 and 32), Tuchman explores various explanations that medieval thinkers attached to the plague: the scientific and the religious. If you have read Lowes' "Time in the Middle Ages," ask students how medieval time schemes influenced "scientific" explanations and how our modes of scientific explanation differ today. You might also ask whether they think religious modes of explanation have changed.
6. In paragraph 12, Tuchman quotes an account left by Brother John Clyn of Kilkenny, Ireland, who "kept a record of what happened lest 'things which should be remembered perish with time and vanish from the memory of those who come after us.'" Discuss this statement as the motivation for writing history, asking students whether they can imagine other motivations.

Suggested Writing Assignments

1. Has human nature changed since the Middle Ages? Do we still respond to disaster in the same ways? Write an essay in which you address these questions using details from Tuchman's account and specific details from a recent disaster you have witnessed and/or read about.
2. In the section of her essay beginning with paragraph 26, Tuchman gives us medieval explanations for the spread of bubonic plague.

After doing research on the topic, write a modern scientific explanation for its spread.

3. Consult one of the sources Tuchman cites at the end of her essay and analyze how Tuchman uses her sources. What does she quote? What does she summarize? How does she shape her material?

4. Read another account of the Black Death, either from an encyclopedia or a history textbook. Compare and contrast that account with Tuchman's, trying to address the following question: What does Tuchman hope to achieve in her account of this fourteenth-century event?

5. Write an essay in response to Analytical Consideration 6, using this and other essays in the "History" section for your evidence.

Additional questions on this essay will be found in the text (NR 766–67, SE 468).

LEO McNAMARA

The State of Ireland

The Norton Reader, p. 767; Shorter Edition, p. 469

Leo McNamara's "The State of Ireland" uses history to explore and explain the current state of affairs in Ireland. His title puns on a second meaning of the word *state*—a political unity, a nation state—and, indeed, this meaning is intricately entwined with the first. You might use McNamara's essay to show students how a writer can use history to illumine current events as well as to raise the difficult question of the extent to which historical understanding can actually help us in resolving current crises. Does it help to know history? we might ask.

Analytical Considerations

1. Why does McNamara begin with a poem and a map rather than dive straight into the history of Ireland? What function do these devices serve?

2. Compare the map of Europe printed at the beginning of McNamara's essay with a modern map. How does cartography affect the way we interpret the "place" of a country?

3. The second section, titled "The History," uses chronology to organize its information. How is the third section, "The Conflict," organized?
4. Several of the paragraphs (e.g., 1 and 3) within "The Conflict" section use the rhetorical mode of comparing and contrasting. Why is McNamara's use of this mode particularly relevant to—even essential for—his American audience?
5. What solution does McNamara imagine for the problem of Ireland? Does the poem he quotes support or complicate his vision?

Suggested Writing Assignments

1. Write an essay about a country or region other than Ireland, using history to illumine its current state of affairs.
2. Write a close analysis of the poem by Seamus Heaney that closes McNamara's essay. Does the poem merely repeat or enforce the points McNamara has made, or does it suggest something additional or different?
3. If you have access to a good map library, compare two or three maps of Ireland, drawn at different periods of history, to suggest how its placement on a map has mirrored its historical and political situation.

CHIEF SEATTLE

Address

The Norton Reader, p. 783; Shorter Edition, p. 475

Chief Seattle, from whom the city of Seattle, Washington, takes its name, was one of the great native American leaders and orators of the nineteenth century. In this speech, which he delivered in acceptance of a treaty with the United States government, Seattle presents two versions of history: the linear, progressive mode of the white man and the more cyclical, reverential history of the red man. Although Seattle does not use phrases like "errand into the wilderness" or "manifest destiny," it is clear that he understands (although disapproves of) the white man's equation of historical progress with the acquisition of land. This essay thus provides a useful alternative to Western concepts of history and a critique of modes of historical thinking we sometimes take for granted.

Analytical Considerations

1. In the opening paragraph, Chief Seattle characterizes the histories of the white and red men with different metaphors. What are they, and what affect do they have? What other metaphors does he use in the course of his speech?
2. Chief Seattle alludes to Christianity and the belief that God is the Father of all men. What seems to be his attitude toward the Christian religion? You might tell your students that Seattle became a Roman Catholic and instituted the custom of holding morning and evening services in his tribe.
3. Seattle suggests that different approaches to history produce different attitudes toward the land. How does he make this argument? Which approach to history do you find more appealing? You might also want to refer your students to another piece by Chief Seattle in "Letter to President Pierce" (NR 626, SE 399).

Suggested Writing Assignments

1. Imagine the response that an American official might have made to Seattle's speech. Write a version of that speech in which you include the white man's view of American history.
2. Compare and contrast this speech of Chief Seattle with his "Letter to President Pierce." Which rhetorical techniques and intellectual concepts are similar? Which are different?
3. Do research on the history of the Dwamish tribe after it signed the treaty of 1854. Were Chief Seattle's predictions of its fate accurate? Write a brief account of the tribe's subsequent history.

HANNAH ARENDT

Denmark and the Jews

The Norton Reader, p. 809; Shorter Edition, p. 478

Perhaps the most important theme of Hannah Arendt's *Eichmann in Jerusalem: A Report on the Banality of Evil* (1963), from which this selection come, is that of the "ordinariness of evil." Adolph Eichmann regarded his role in the infamous Nazi "final solution to the Jewish question" as that of a "functionary." At his trial in Jerusalem, he most regretted having been ill-used by superiors. According to Arendt, his inability to acknowledge personal blame was not extraordinary or abnormal, for evil apparently loses its character as evil when it is assimilated into the normal routine of living and working.

It is against this background that Arendt sets the Danish reaction to the Nazi program of destruction. In this selection Arendt contends that the Danes provided the "only case we know of in which the Nazis met with *open* native resistance" (paragraph 17). This point (and several others in her book) have been criticized by other observers. What Arendt does to marshal support for her views is fill her discussion with an overwhelming number of facts and statistics that lend an air of authority to *all* that she says. Moreover, she studiously avoids emotionalism in presenting her views. Whether or not one wholly accepts Arendt's opinion, her general views (about the Danes, about the "ordinariness" of evil) provide fascinating vantage points for discussion.

Analytical Considerations

1. "Denmark and the Jews" is partially narrative in organization. Does the narrative have a climax? Where does it occur? What is the effect of being told the implications of the story before actually learning the story?
2. The tendency to think the Danes moral heroes seems an inevitable effect of this essay. Is there evidence that Arendt tries to temper this opinion, to make us see the Danes as something other than or as less than heroes? (This question should not imply seeing them as villains.)
3. Read the essay carefully for evidence of Arendt's bitterness about the history and fate of European Jews. What are her chief means of controlling this bitterness so that its appearance is effective?
4. Distinguish the facts in Arendt's essay from the views of the author. Then decide how well the facts support the views. In all cases can you clearly say that Arendt's ideas have been drawn by valid induction?
5. Evaluate the final paragraph of "Denmark and the Jews." Which statements in the paragraph are matters of record? Which are matters of contention? How well are the matters of contention prepared for by preceding sections?
6. Why does Arendt describe the Danes as a nation or a group instead of focusing on individuals? In view of her purpose, is there a rhetorical advantage in so viewing them?
7. Does Arendt regard her subject as primarily a moral, an ethical, or a

historical one? If so, what facets of the discussion suggest this view? How valid as history is Arendt's moral approach to her subject?

Suggested Writing Assignments

1. If Nazis like Eichmann exhibit the "ordinariness of evil," then the Danes exhibit the "ordinariness of good." Drawing from your own experience, write an essay in which you support, refute, or evaluate this assertion.
2. Compare Arendt's ideas on "resistance based on principle" and "nonviolent action" with Martin Luther King's in "Letter from Birmingham Jail" (NR 886, SE 538).
3. Using "Denmark and the Jews" as a basis, construct a code of conduct for nonviolent resistance to any unjust authority or unjust policy.
4. Write a historical narrative of some person or group who in some vital or violent controversy held to principle and proved to be exceptional.

FRANCES FITZGERALD

Rewriting American History

The Norton Reader, p. 818; Shorter Edition, p. 483

Frances FitzGerald is a talented journalist, popularly known for her account of the Vietnam War *Fire in the Lake*. The essay "Rewriting American History" is actually one of three parts of a long essay that appeared serially in the *New Yorker* in the winter of 1979 and was later included in her book *America Revised*. This segment is, for the most part, a highly detailed comparison and contrast between history textbooks of the 1950s and contemporary history texts. Interesting in their own right, the comparison and contrast lead nevertheless to what may interest the reader even more: general commentary on the nature of history as a discipline, which accounts for the changes in texts and history, and personal remarks about the mind's yearning for permanence and order.

Analytical Considerations

1. Ask students to summarize FitzGerald's essay in one paragraph,

then ask several students to read their paragraphs aloud. From the similarities and differences, begin a discussion about the points most easily grasped, those less easily grasped, and why.

2. What is FitzGerald's understanding of "history"?

3. Why do human beings need to create "history"?

4. FitzGerald relies mainly on the mode of comparing and contrasting to show how American history has been "rewritten." By focusing on two paragraphs, perhaps paragraphs 4 and 9, ask students to discuss how the comparison and contrast work.

5. Analyze any single section of "Rewriting American History" to show how FitzGerald defines by example. Possibilities include the section on the political diversity of textbooks today and the section on the physical appearance of textbooks today.

6. Explain how FitzGerald's essay uses the strategy of defining by analysis as well as defining by example and defining by comparing and contrasting. Is it common for these strategies to work together so that it becomes difficult to isolate one from another?

7. Evaluate the design and impact of FitzGerald's conclusion.

8. Ask students if FitzGerald's essay implies that we will never be able to (re)construct history, that we will be able to produce only histories that have no permanent place or value.

Suggested Writing Assignments

1. Write an essay based on comparing and contrasting the same episode from American history as presented in three textbooks, each written during a different decade; be certain to select texts written for the same grade level.

2. To what extent do history textbooks, or any other history books, present "truths"? Use your own ideas as well as ideas from other writers in this section.

3. Has the process of rewriting American history taken much of the romance and myth from the subject. Is that good or bad or both?

Additional questions on this essay will be found in the text (NR 824–25, SE 489–90).

JOAN DIDION

On Keeping a Notebook

The Norton Reader, p. 680; Shorter Edition, p. 490

From an entry in her own notebook, Joan Didion writes about the process of reconstructing—not only the event recorded in her notebook but also herself. This essay provides an unusual opportunity to observe the nonfiction writer at work, exploring one aspect of her art and a significant dimension of herself. Writing enables Didion to discover who she is and how she has come to be that person. Reviewing entries in her notebook allows her to "keep on nodding terms with the people [she] used to be." This essay, a reflective commentary on the significance of journal keeping, attempts to be honest, uncompromising, and challenging.

Analytical Considerations

1. Why does Didion keep a notebook? What purpose do the "bits of the mind's string too short to use" (paragraph 11) have for her?
2. At what point does the reader realize that the woman in the plaid dress is Didion herself? Why does Didion describe herself in the third person? How does this objective form of description, used in her notebook, help Didion understand herself and her situation?
3. What is the function of the questions in paragraph 4? Are they a substitute for a thesis?
4. Ask students whether they agree with Didion when she says, "I think we are well advised to keep on nodding terms with the people we used to be whether we find them attractive company or not" (paragraph 16).
5. Why does the distinction between what happened and what might have happened not matter for Didion? What does it tell us about the reconstructive powers of memory?
6. In what sense(s) is the process of keeping and working from a notebook like the process of writing history? In what sense(s) is it different?
7. Didion's essay is filled with details from her notebook. Barbara Tuchman's essay "'This is the End of the World': The Black Death" (NR 754, G 131) is also filled with details. Ask students to analyze how these details are similar and different, moving toward an

understanding of how and why a historian selects and shapes her material.

8. In an essay titled "Why I Write," Didion noted, "I write entirely to find out what I'm thinking, what I'm looking at, what I see and what it means." In the same essay, she reveals that for her "certain images shimmer" and that these images determine the "arrangement of words." Apply these comments to "On Keeping a Notebook" as well as to "On Going Home" (NR 31, SE 23). With some guided discussion, students should be able to develop a sense of Didion's literary esthetic and practice. You might also assign an essay titled "Joan Didion: One Writer's Sense of Style and Purpose."

Suggested Writing Assignments

1. Keep a notebook for a week or so; carry it with you and record what you like. At the end of the week review it, then write an analysis and commentary on your notebook. Do you share the same interests and motives in writing as Didion?

2. Write an essay in response to Didion's observation: "we are well advised to keep on nodding terms with the people we used to be whether we find them attractive company or not" (paragraph 16).

3. Compare and contrast the details Didion includes with the details from a historian's essay—for example, Tuchman's "'This Is the End of the World': The Black Death." How does the historian's purpose call forth different—and a different use of—details?

Additional questions on this essay will be found in the text (NR 74, SE 496).

EDWARD HALLETT CARR

The Historian and His Facts

The Norton Reader, p. 883; Shorter Edition, p. 497

Edward Hallett Carr's "The Historian and His Facts" is a classic essay in the field of historiography. Charles Kay Smith's *Styles and Structures* (1974) has informed my [Robert E. Hosmer's] teaching of this essay for years, and so, with his kind permission, I offer a condensed version of it. My summary does not do justice to the fullness of Smith's thought; I encourage you to read Chapter 13 of Smith's book yourself.

Carr's essay illustrates the classical rhetoric of synthesis. First, he presents the nineteenth-century assumption that history is a series of self-evident inductions based on all available facts (thesis); then he offers the twentieth-century assumption that history has no objective facts but consists rather of interpretation; finally, rejecting both, he creates a synthesis of the two by asserting that history is a tension or process of interaction between fact and interpretation. Smith calls Carr's method of organizing his writing "assumptive style," and that is the clearest way of getting to the heart of "The Historian and His Facts."

Analytical Considerations

1. Textual clues indicate that "The Historian and His Facts" was originally given as a public lecture at Oxford University. What affect might the occasion have had on Carr's style and organization?
2. How does Carr define *history* in this essay? Would his definition be compatible with Frances FitzGerald's as indicated in "Rewriting American History" (NR 818, SE 483)?
3. What does the narrative of Stresemann's papers illustrate?
4. How does Carr develop and support thesis, antithesis, and synthesis in "The Historian and His Facts"?
5. Carr does not write what students might consider standard history (nor, for that matter, do the great historians like Thucydides, Fernand Braudel, and Michel Foucault). One distinguishing feature of Carr's essay is his use of metaphor. Ask students where and how he uses metaphor (e.g., the fish market metaphor, theological metaphor, biblical metaphor). What is the effect of metaphorical language in an essay on historiography? What other historians in this section rely on metaphorical language?

Suggested Writing Assignments

1. Write an essay about how FitzGerald's "Rewriting American History" could be read as a response to Carr, or write an essay comparing and contrasting FitzGerald's and Carr's senses of "history."
2. Write an essay of definition for an important and disputed term,

following the thesis-antithesis-synthesis pattern used by Carr in "The Historian and His Facts."

3. Respond to the question "What is history?" in an essay of your own.

Additional questions on this essay will be found in the text (NR 849, SE 513).

POLITICS AND GOVERNMENT

NICCOLÒ MACHIAVELLI

The Morals of the Prince

The Norton Reader, p. 901; Shorter Edition, p. 514

Niccolò Machiavelli, the Florentine whose political treatise *The Prince* was published in 1513, acquired in his time a scandalous reputation: He was "Old Nick" (or Satan), who held the diabolical doctrine that the end justifies the means. His reputation was largely established by the chapters on "The Morals of the Prince" reprinted in *The Norton Reader*. Students should notice how Machiavelli is aware of making a different and controversial case, of writing about the *is*— "the way we really live"—rather than the *ought*—"the way we ought to live" (paragraph 1). Political treatises of Machiavelli's time were usually utopian. Machiavelli's is not, and consequently, as he announces, he has something new to say. Today we might speak of his politics as *realpolitik*, a word derived from German that means a politics based on practical and material rather than on theoretical and ethical considerations.

You might use "The Morals of the Prince" to exemplify shifting boundaries between idealism and realism, realism and cynicism: We can pretty much agree on their definitions, but when we come to apply them, what one person takes to be realistic another person can take to be cynical. Nevertheless, Machiavelli appears to present his argument with intent to shock. While it may be realistic to present the dangers of virtue in a world in which people are "a sad lot, and keep no faith with you" (paragraph 14), it is surely cynical to argue that the appearance of virtue is better than virtue itself. Students should notice the frequent antitheses in Machiavelli's argument—the qualities in a prince that elicit praise or blame (paragraph 2) and the chapter headings in which he opposes liberality to stinginess, cruelty to clemency, and love to fear—and the way he values and transvalues these opposed terms.

Analytical Considerations

1. One feature of Machiavelli's style is his use of aphorisms, that is, terse formulations of truths and beliefs. You might ask students to gather a number of them and describe how Machiavelli uses them

and to what effect or effects.

2. What are Machiavelli's customary sources of examples? How frequently does he use them? How extensively does he explain them?

3. Man, in the Renaissance chain of being, stands between beasts and angels. You might have students look at paragraphs 14 and 15, in which Machiavelli proposes as models for imitation the fox and the lion. How does his choice of metaphor contribute to his argument?

Suggested Writing Assignments

1. Write an essay defining "Machiavellian" by applying it to and illustrating it with examples from contemporary politics.

2. Do library research on the politics of Florence during Machiavelli's life (on the way Florentines really lived) and write an essay in which you consider *The Prince* as a response to local conditions.

3. Write an essay in which you explain the positions Machiavelli takes concerning the nature of man, the function of government, and the relationship between morality and political life in "The Morals of the Prince."

4. See also Suggested Writing Assignments 2 and 3 for "The Declaration of Independence" (153–54).

Additional questions on this essay will be found in the text (NR 908, SE 521).

JONATHAN SWIFT

A Modest Proposal

The Norton Reader, p. 878; Shorter Edition, p. 522

"A Modest Proposal" is often anthologized as a brilliant example of sustained irony. It is also shocking: You might ask students to read Samuel Clemens' "Advice to Youth" (NR 662, SE 411) to contrast the tameness of Clemens' irony with the savagery of Swift's. Swift violates one of our strongest prohibitions, against eating human flesh. Moreover, he disquietingly juxtaposes the reasonable voice of his putative author (or invented persona) and his horrifying proposals, horrifying to us as readers but apparently not horrifying their proposer. The author's "modest proposal" can perhaps be entertained as logically consistent. But because it engages feeling and morality, it is indefensible. Swift's juxtaposition of reasonableness and horror, you will probably need to remind students, is ironic: While the putative author of "A Modest Proposal" says one thing, Swift, the implied author, must mean another.

You will need to say something about Irish poverty in 1729, when Swift published "A Modest Proposal," and its historical causes. Irony over time is problematic: You might have students look at paragraphs 29 and 30, Swift's "other expedients," which will suggest some of the things Swift's audience knew that we no longer know. You might also remind them that, if Swift had been anxious to prevent a literal reading, he would have included these expedients earlier; they serve here to remind readers, rather than to inform them, of what Swift himself would propose.

Analytical Considerations

1. You might begin by having students identify examples of the reasonable voice of Swift's putative author: The name of the essay itself comes to mind, as well as its mathematical calculations and culinary considerations.
2. Ask students to describe how Swift's putative author characterizes himself by his style. If style is the man, what kind of man are we listening to?
3. Although Swift's primary concerns are economic, issues of population control also run through "A Modest Proposal." What do the putative author's proposals indicate about his views of sexuality and reproduction? Can we infer Swift's proposals and his views of sexuality and reproduction from them? You will want to suggest ways in which time (and changing sexual and reproductive practices) destabilizes Swift's irony with respect to population control more than with respect to economic policy.

Suggested Writing Assignments

1. Write a Swiftian satire of your own on some situation that you think calls for a change in policy. Be sure, as Swift does, to anticipate probable objections to your proposal.
2. Write an essay in which you consider your responses to "A Modest Proposal." Some readers have found Swift's irony too shocking, so strong as to detract from his really quite sensible proposals for reform. Does his literary form subvert his purposes or serve them? How?

Additional questions on this essay will be found in the text (NR 885–86, SE 529).

JAMES THURBER

The Rabbits Who Caused All the Trouble

The Norton Reader, p. 908; Shorter Edition, p. 530

Students will enjoy "The Rabbits Who Caused All the Trouble," although many of them will not know the Aesopian fables Thurber imitates and parodies; they are more likely to know George Orwell's *Animal Farm*. You might well distribute a couple of Aesop's fables before discussing Thurber's, so that students will be able to compare the doggedly serious Aesopian morals with Thurber's witty inversions of them.

Robert Scholes makes several useful points about fables in *Textual Power* (1985). Two of these are useful for discussing Thurber (and other parables in NR 1153–65): (1) We read a parable for story; we interpret it for meaning and (2) the moral attached by the author may be *a* meaning, but is not *the* meaning. Parables are polysemous—that is, they contain multiple meanings.

Analytical Considerations

1. Ask students to write a serious Aesopian moral for Thurber's fable.
2. You might ask students how they know the politics of the animals represent human politics. (It's good to remind them of their textual know-how whenever possible.)
3. "The Rabbits Who Caused All the Trouble" was published 1955, more than over thirty-five years ago. What political situations might Thurber's audience have brought to their interpretations of it? Are there more recent situations that we can bring to our interpretations of it?

Suggested Writing Assignments

1. Write an essay in which you interpret "The Rabbits Who Caused All the Trouble" or another of Thurber's fables for its meanings.
2. Consider an alternate, "serious" moral for "The Rabbits Who Caused All the Trouble," for example, Be wary at all times. Write

an essay in which you argue for one moral over another. Be sure to make explicit your criteria for judging morals.
3. Write an animal fable of your own.

GEORGE ORWELL

Shooting an Elephant

The Norton Reader, p. 850; Shorter Edition, p. 531

George Orwell's "Shooting an Elephant" is a classic example of an essay in which the author uses a personal experience to illuminate an institution or an abstraction: here, the experience of shooting an elephant and the British Raj (the imperial government of India and Burma) or colonialism itself. Orwell carefully and precisely renders setting, action, and character (himself) by developing his responses, feelings, and thoughts with novelistic density. He braids into the narrative his personal and general reflections on colonialism rather than holding them off until the conclusion, so that the essay ends with his reflecting on the personal dimensions of the experience: "I often wondered whether any of the others grasped that I had done it solely to avoid looking like a fool" (paragraph 14). Orwell, whom students are likely to know as the author of *Animal Farm* and *1984*, served in the British police force in Burma after leaving school. The experience heightened his political consciousness.

You may need to remind students that "Shooting an Elephant" is also an essay about role-playing, in particular, about how the expectations of others can force us to behave in ways that we do not choose and as selves other than the selves we think we are, worse selves, as in this essay, and probably better selves as well. What is the educative function of role-playing in "Shooting an Elephant"?

Analytical Considerations

1. Ask students why Orwell shot the elephant. Their accounting for the occasion and his multiple motives will demonstrate the novelistic elements of his narrative and help them see the value of dense rendering and how it can be done.
2. Students should consider Orwell's role-playing and their own. Can they provide serious (rather than trivial) examples of the latter, both of worse and of better selves? Is role-playing always educational?

Suggested Writing Assignments

1. Rewrite Orwell's shooting an elephant from the point of view of one of the Burmese natives.
2. Write an essay about an experience that illuminated an institution or an abstraction.
3. Use Orwell's experience of role-playing or your own to argue against Willard Gaylin's denial of inner selves and the possibility of a split between inner and outer selves. See "What You See Is the Real You" (NR 675, SE 414).

Additional questions on this essay will be found in the text (NR 856–57, SE 537–38).

MARTIN LUTHER KING, JR.

Letter from Birmingham Jail

The Norton Reader, p. 886; Shorter Edition, p. 538

Martin Luther King, Jr., was the most important figure in the American civil rights movement before his assassination in 1968, at the age of thirty-nine. He participated in the Montgomery, Alabama, bus boycott in 1966 (see paragraph 35) and in the Birmingham, Alabama, demonstrations in 1963, where he was arrested along with many other demonstrators. "Letter from Birmingham Jail" he wrote in response to a published statement by eight Birmingham clergymen who supported the goals of the civil rights movement but criticized King for his "unwise and untimely" activism.

King uses Christian doctrine and Christian belief to make common cause with the white clergymen to whom he addresses his letter: See his reference to the Black Muslim movement and its repudiation of Christianity (paragraph 27). You can use his reference to Black Muslim bitterness and hatred to lead into a discussion of his nonviolent activism. Central to his justification of activism—"civil disobedience"—is his distinction between just and unjust laws (paragraphs 15 to 20). You might ask students to summarize this distinction and his applications of it.

Analytical Considerations

1. You might ask students to explain the paradox of King's both urging obedience to the law, namely, the 1954 Supreme Court decision outlawing segregation in public schools, and breaking it.
2. Do your students know about other recent instances of civil disobedience other than those associated with the civil rights movement? You may have to explain resistance to the war in Vietnam, unless you have older students in your class. More recent instances would include resistance to the use of nuclear power, both peaceful and military.
3. King, who expresses his disappointment with whites who call themselves moderates, alternately characterizes himself as moderate and extremist. You might ask students to look at instances of both and the kinds of behavior to which he attaches these labels. Which characterization do they think was more accurate in 1963, which more accurate today?

Suggested Writing Assignments

1. Imagine an unjust law that, to you, would justify civil disobedience. Describe the law, the form your resistance would take, and the penalties you would expect to incur. Or, if you can't see yourself engaging in civil disobedience, imagine an unjust law and the form someone else's resistance to it would take, and then write a letter in which you try to convince this person to obey rather than to resist.
2. Do library research on Mahatma Gandhi and his doctrine of nonviolent resistance. Then, on the basis of King's "Letter from Birmingham Jail," analyze similarities and differences between Gandhi's and King's ideas about and uses of nonviolent resistance.
3. King calls into question, in the context of events in Birmingham, "the strangely irrational notion that there is something in the very flow of time that will inevitably cure all ills" (paragraph 26). Is this an "irrational notion"? Supply two or three other contexts in which the notion might figure and write an essay in which you reconsider King's generalization.

STEPHEN HUME

The Spirit Weeps

The Norton Reader, p. 857; Shorter Edition, p. 552

Stephen Hume is a Canadian journalist, essayist, and poet. The occasion of this essay, "The Spirit Weeps," he explains in paragraphs 1 to 11; its title inverts the title of the controversial exhibit of the art of Canadian Indians, "The Spirit Sings." From the occasion and the objects on display Hume moves back in time to describe various indignities inflicted on particular Indian nations and the genocidal campaigns of Canadians against the aboriginal inhabitants of their land. Students should be able to see how, in the first part of the essay, Hume puts together historical information that he undoubtedly has researched. In the second part of his essay, however, he turns from history to current events through a response to the exhibit (paragraphs 30 to 33): "it's all in the past." With this direct quotation he alters his mode from narrative to argument: "Tell it," "Tell it," "Tell it" (paragraphs 34 through 37).

Hume's shift enables him to describe present indignities inflicted on the aborigines and Canadians' continuing indifference and hostility toward them. In consequence, students should question the conclusion to his essay, that the first act of every Canadian prime minister should be to pray for national forgiveness. Hume prescribes symbolic rather than real remedies, penance for the past rather than amelioration for the present.

Analytical Considerations

1. To whom are the imperatives of paragraphs 33 to 36 addressed?
2. What other possibilities are there for ending this essay? Ask students to speculate about why Hume stays with the symbolic.

Suggested Writing Assignments

1. Do additional library research on one or more of the Canadian Indian nations Hume mentions or on one or more American Indian nations; you might, for example, investigate the Kiowa nation that F. Scott Momaday talks about in "The Way to Rainy Mountain" (NR 158, SE 80). Write a straightforward account of their extinction or near extinction, an emotional account, or both.

2. Do library research on at least one recent controversy over native American sacred artifacts in art or ethnographic museums. Write a short paper outlining the issues and the problems of resolving them.

3. "Art cannot be detached from the social and historical matrix in which it originates, however much museum curators might desire to do so in the interest of neat classification and compartmentalized analysis" (paragraph 4). This generalization is applicable to the art Hume describes; is it applicable to all art, as Hume seems to claim? In a short essay, discuss its relevance to an exhibit in a museum you are familiar with, or go look at an exhibit in a local museum. With respect to this exhibit, *do* museums attempt to reattach art to its social and historical matrix and how? If they don't, how might they attempt to reattach it?

THOMAS JEFFERSON

Original Draft of the Declaration of Independence

The Norton Reader, p. 924; Shorter Edition, p. 563

and

THOMAS JEFFERSON AND OTHERS

The Declaration of Independence

The Norton Reader, p. 928; Shorter Edition, p. 567

These two drafts of "The Declaration of Independence"—the first, Jefferson's preliminary draft, and the second, the final draft as printed—may provoke students into a fresh reading of a text whose familiarity dulls attention. The preliminary draft is a transcription of a copy in Jefferson's hand (in the Library of Congress), with illegible passages taken from a transcription made by John Adams and missing passages, presumably added later, taken from a copy Jefferson made for George Wythe (in the New York Public Library). We do not know how many drafts and revisions preceded it; we do know that Jefferson consulted with several people, among them Benjamin Franklin and John Adams. This preliminary draft was edited somewhat by members of the Second Continental Congress and in large measure, undoubtedly, by Jefferson himself.

Students should notice that the three-part structure of the preliminary and final drafts is the same: Jefferson enunciates a series of principles concerning human nature and the function of government, rehearses the offenses against them by George III, and proclaims the political connection between the American colonies and the kings of Great Britain dissolved. The structure is derived from the syllogism: a major premise, a minor premise, and a conclusion. The logic is deductive: given the principles, which Jefferson calls "sacred & undeniable" in the preliminary draft, "self-evident" in the final, and given the facts, the conclusion follows ineluctably.

These two versions of "The Declaration of Independence" illustrate the final revision procedures of an experienced writer. With his argumentative structure and his particulars in place, Jefferson revises at the paragraph and sentence level. Chiefly he prunes and tightens: He recognizes that he has been somewhat overinclusive in his exemplification, somewhat clumsy in his sentences, and long-winded in using more words than he needs, to say what he needs to say. While his language in the final draft is more direct and simple, his sentence structure, especially with respect to repetition and balance, is more artful. The spelling and punctuation of the final draft have, of course, been made consistent.

Analytical Considerations

1. You might ask students to work on the first or second sections of "The Declaration of Independence," noting what Jefferson has pruned and reconstructing, insofar as they can, the thinking behind the omissions.

2. Ask them, individually or in groups, to compare particular sentences in which Jefferson has simplified his language and heightened his sentence structure with repetition and balance. You might also ask them to "modernize" these sentences by loosening repetition and balance without reverting to Jefferson's original sentence structure.

Suggested Writing Assignments

1. Write an essay in which you explain the positions Jefferson takes concerning the nature of man, the function of government, and the relationship between morality and political life in "The Declaration of Independence." What assumptions are necessary to make these positions, as he says in the final draft, "self-evident"?

2. Write a comparison of Jefferson's positions concerning the nature of man, the function of government, and the relationship between

morality and political life in "The Declaration of Independence" and Niccolò Machiavelli's positions in "The Morals of the Prince" (NR 901, SE 514). In addition, compare their assumptions.

3. Are you a Jeffersonian or a Machiavellian? Explain. (Discussion of the material and procedures of Suggested Writing Assignments 1 and 2 should probably precede this assignment.)

4. Write an argument on a topic of your choice in which you use the three-part structure of a syllogism.

Additional questions on these essays will be found in the text (NR 931–32, SE 570).

ABRAHAM LINCOLN

Second Inaugural Address

The Norton Reader, p. 922; Shorter Edition, p. 571

Abraham Lincoln's "Second Inaugural Address" is a piece of ceremonial discourse required by the occasion of Lincoln's second inauguration; it is formal in tone and diction, also as required by the occasion. Like Martin Luther King, Jr., Lincoln assumes Christian belief even while pointing out that, although North and South "read the same Bible, and pray to the same God," neither has evidence of God's unqualified favor. Lincoln's strategy is to invite reconciliation with, not alienation of, the South while keeping up the resolve of the North in fighting for a just cause.

Analytical Considerations

1. You might remind students that Lincoln reviews four years in the course of this brief address. What events does he select, and what pattern does he see in them?

2. Lincoln uses three types of rhetorical appeal in this address: logical, emotional, and ethical. Ask students to identify examples of each. Which do they find most effective? Which do they think Lincoln's audience found most effective?

3. While Lincoln tries to speak to both North and South, students probably will not find him hypocritical or slippery. You might encourage students to a closer reading of the address by suggesting

that he might be. Ask them to consider how he presents himself as honest and his purpose as single-minded.

Suggested Writing Assignments

1. Write an essay in which you compare Lincoln's "Second Inaugural Address" with John F. Kennedy's first (and only) inaugural address in 1961. Compare both content, rhetoric, and audience.
2. Do library research on the beginning of Lincoln's second term as president and write an essay in which you consider his "Second Inaugural Address" as a response to local conditions.

E. B. WHITE

Democracy

The Norton Reader, p. 934; Shorter Edition, p. 572

In this short essay, which originally appeared in the *New Yorker*, E. B. White writes, on request (he explains the circumstances in the essay), about a well-worn topic. He makes it fresh by providing a series of examples that function as metaphors, technically as synecdoches, or figures of speech in which a part stands for the whole. He provides images and avoids abstractions. Presumably the War Board, which asked him to write about "The Meaning of Democracy" in 1943 (during World War II), expected a patriotic response. Is White's response patriotic, or is it flip? Ask students to be explicit about the grounds of their answers; encourage variety and disagreement.

Analytical Considerations

1. White creates his definition with a series of examples. You might ask students to determine if a principle orders them or if they are random.
2. Ask students to consider the date of composition: 1943. Are any of White's examples dated? Can they suggest more contemporary substitutes?
3. Ask students to consider an abstraction they might be asked to define in an examination in another course. Have them, probably in groups, construct answers in the manner of E. B. White and consider

their professors' probable reactions. (You might dare them to try such an answer on an examination.)

Suggested Writing Assignments

1. Write a definition of *democracy* or some comparable abstraction in the manner of E. B. White, taking examples familiar to you.
2. Imagine yourself a member of the War Board who finds White's response unpatriotically flip and write him a letter explaining why the War Board declines to use it. Or imagine yourself a member of the War Board who finds White's response particularly useful and write him a letter thanking him for it. Or write both letters.

Additional questions on this essay will be found in the text (NR 934–35, SE 573)

SCIENCE

HORACE FREELAND JUDSON

The Rage to Know

The Norton Reader, p. 942; Shorter Edition, p. 574

Unlike the other authors whose essays appear in this section of
The Norton Reader, Horace Freeland Judson is a journalist who
specializes in writing about science rather than a scientist. His coming
to science secondhand is evidenced by the number of quotations in
"The Rage to Know": He has asked scientists about their motives and
practices and excerpted (from presumably longer interviews) telling
quotations. He does not, however, merely report what scientists say;
he fits it into his own interpretive structure. Scientists are motivated
by what he calls "the rage to know" and proceed by imagination and
intuition as well as by data gathering and verification.

In general, Judson presents science as a rather exalted activity and
scientists as rather exalted beings in search of order, meaning, and
beauty. While he quotes Francis Bacon to the effect that knowledge is
power (paragraph 18) and discusses links between science and
technology, he quickly returns to the disinterestedness of scientists.
His essay appeared in the *Atlantic Monthly* in 1980; the decade since
has produced a critique of science that Judson does not consider.
Students may find Judson perversely innocent, or you may. To
encourage criticism, have them read Terry Tempest Williams' "The
Clan of One-Breasted Women" (NR 639, SE 401) and Stephen Jay
Gould's "Scientific Error" (NR 1030, SE 634). Nevertheless, Judson's
essay contains points about scientific communities and scientific
writing useful in considering other essays in this section.

Analytical Considerations

1. You might direct students to the various accounts of how thinking
proceeds and what it feels like in "A Rage to Know." Do any of
them describe an experience analogous to one of theirs? Why is it
so hard to describe thinking?
2. Science, Judson claims, is "our century's art" (paragraph 18). This
claim will probably take some explaining; even Judson recognizes
that in our time art is undervalued (paragraph 21). You might try

working back and forth from his conception of the scientist in paragraphs 18 to 23 to the conception of the artist he hearkens back to.

Suggested Writing Assignments

1. Think about an instance in which you came to understand something, in which your experience approximated "a moment of pure scientific perception" (paragraph 1). Write an essay in which you describe and analyze it. You may use Judson's "The Rage to Know" or ignore it.

2. Look again at Judson's description of the discovery of DNA (paragraph 6) and then read James D. Watson's *The Double Helix* (1969). Watson's account of the less-than-disinterested process of discovery shocked—and was perhaps intended to shock. Write an essay in which you consider Watson's account in relation to Judson's.

3. Judson quotes Rosalind Franklin, a crystallographer who worked with Watson, to the effect that science is fun. Her career may serve to illustrate Evelyn Fox Keller's contention that it is less fun for women than for men; see "Women in Science: A Social Analysis" (NR 1020, SE 625). Read Anne Sayres' biography, *Rosalind Franklin and DNA* (1975) and write an essay in which you discuss science as a gendered practice.

4. Choose a subject about which you have limited first-hand experience but, in preparation for writing, locate two or three people with firsthand experience. The subject can be close to home: a course or a school or social event. Interview your authorities and use what they say to write your own description and analysis. You might append a paragraph in which you discuss what you include and exclude from your interviews.

Additional questions on this essay will be found in the text (NR 952, SE 584).

NIKO TINBERGEN

The Bee-Hunters of Hulshorst

The Norton Reader, p. 953; Shorter Edition, p. 585

In "The Rage to Know" (NR 924, SE 574), Horace Freeland Judson quotes Sir Peter Medawar: "'What scientists *do* has never been the subject of a scientific . . . inquiry. It is no use looking to scientific "papers," for they not merely conceal but actively misrepresent the reasoning that goes into the work they describe'" (paragraph 5). "The Bee-Hunters of Hulshorst" is a personal account rather than a scientific inquiry. Written in retrospect, it may not represent the actual reasoning that went into Niko Tinbergen's study of the bee-hunting wasps, but it does not, by casting the results of that study into the standard form of a scientific report, misrepresent it. (For a scientific report, see John Henry Sloan et al., "Handgun Regulations, Crime, Assaults, and Homicide: A Tale of Two Cities" (NR 996, SE 598). The genesis of "The Bee-Hunters of Hulshorst," from which these passages are taken, is casual: Tinbergen's subject is not scientific inquiry but rather his experiences at his parents' vacation home in The Netherlands. Students may notice the gaps and the unexplained shift (beginning in paragraph 28) from Tinbergen the solitary researcher (*I*) to a member of what must be a team (*we*). Tinbergen reveals how one scientist located a topic for a doctoral dissertation through, on the face of it, happenstance.

In scientific papers, researchers obliterate themselves. Tinbergen is very much present in this account and inquires into his involvement: "it is always worth observing oneself as well as the animals," he writes (paragraph 23). The involvement he records may surprise students. His presence is also visible in his attributing to the wasps human responses and motives; paragraphs 18 and 19 include a good example. Probably some degree of anthropomorphizing is inevitable, inasmuch as our vocabulary for describing behavior is drawn from descriptions of our own. Nevertheless, students may feel, and rightly, that Tinbergen's descriptions markedly humanize the wasps.

Analytic Considerations

1. Does Tinbergen overstate the casualness of his locating a research problem? You might ask students to read both Horace Freeland Judson's "The Rage to Know" and Jacob Bronowski's "The Nature

of Scientific Reasoning" (NR 942, SE 574) and speculate about Tinbergen's omissions.

2. You might ask students if it makes a difference to their reading of "The Bee-Hunters of Hulshorst" to know that Tinbergen won a Nobel Prize.

3. Horace Freeland Judson, in "The Rage to Know," offers a number of reasons for doing science (paragraph 6). To what extent do these figure in Tinbergen's account?

4. See Sir Peter Medawar's comment, quoted by Horace Freeland Judson in "The Rage to Know": "'Scientists are building explanatory structures, *telling stories* which are scrupulously tested to see if they are stories about real life'" (paragraph 5). Does it describe Tinbergen's procedures?

5. After looking at the anthropomorphizing vocabulary of paragraphs 18 and 19, you might ask students, perhaps working in groups, to find additional examples.

6. After looking at the anthropomorphizing vocabulary of paragraphs 18 and 19, you might ask students, again working in groups, to rewrite portions of them as stripped as possible of anthropomorphizing language.

Suggested Writing Assignments

1. Locate one of Tinbergen's scientific reports on the bee-hunting wasps of Hulshorst, or another of his scientific reports, or a scientific report written by another animal behaviorist. Write an essay on the structure of the report, how it obliterates the researcher, and how it represents or misrepresents the reasoning that went into the inquiry.

2. Locate one of Tinbergen's scientific reports on the bee-hunting wasps of Hulshorst, or another of his scientific reports, or a scientific report written by another animal behaviorist. Look carefully at and write an analysis of what you identify as its anthropomorphizing vocabulary. You may wish to compare it with "The Bee-Hunters of Hulshorst."

Additional questions on this essay will be found in text (NR 965, SE 597).

Handgun Regulations, Crime, Assaults, and Homicide:
A Tale of Two Cities

The Norton Reader, p. 966; Shorter Edition, p. 598

"Handgun Regulations, Crime, Assaults, and Homicide" is a scientific report written by a team of nine researchers, John Henry Sloan and eight others comprehended under "et al." They are listed in an order that represents their relative importance; multiple researchers (and multiple authors) are the rule in scientific research today. The report, published in the *New England Journal of Medicine*, is addressed to professional colleagues. It follows a prescribed form, with sections headed "Abstract," "Methods," "Results," "Discussion," and "References"; only the introductory section, between "Abstract" and "Methods," lacks a heading; in some scientific reports it is labeled "Background" or "Review of Literature." Information, whenever possible, is expressed mathematically. The report contains four tables and three figures. Its prose is generally agentless: The researchers are largely invisible (although on occasion they refer to themselves as *we*) and so are the people who commit crimes. The title is long, exact, clumsy; the literary allusion in the subtitle, to Dickens' *A Tale of Two Cities*, is unusual.

It is possible to discuss the features of scientific reporting without a close reading of Sloan et al. See, for example, Sir Peter Medawar as quoted in Horace Freeland Judson's "The Rage to Know" (NR 942, SE 574): Scientific reports "'not merely conceal but actively misrepresent the reasoning that goes into the work they describe'" (paragraph 5). How do the sections of the report represent the research of Sloan et al. and how do they misrepresent it?

Close reading of "Handgun Regulations, Crime, Assaults, and Homicide" will demonstrate how scientific reporting neglects to contextualize and explain, both of which experienced writers of other kinds of prose are careful to do. Consequently, the report demands unusually active attention. You might, to start, have students look closely at Table 1. What does it claim about comparablity, and what are its anomalies? How (and where) do Sloan et al. take them into account? If this kind of attention seems useful, continue with Analytical Considerations 3 and 4.

"Handgun Regulations, Crime, Assaults, and Homicide" is the most extensively annotated selection in *The Norton Reader:* In some sections, virtually every sentence is followed by a number or numbers. You may want to explain the system; more important, you should discuss how scientists in particular (and academic researchers in general) locate their research with reference to other research.

Analytical Considerations

1. Ask students to describe the differences between a table and a figure. You might also ask them to consider the uses of each.
2. You might look at the examples of agentless prose in paragraph 7. For the suppression of researchers: "To date, no study"; for the suppression of people who commit crimes: "the rates of gun ownership are high but homicides are relatively uncommon." You might ask students to locate additional examples of agentless prose.
3. Tables 3 and 4 represent 1980–1986; Figure 1 contains a line between 1983/1984 and 1986. What is the reason for these variations, and where in the report is it explained?
4. The discussion section concludes with three limitations that "warrant comment." What are they, and how do they qualify the results of Sloan et al.'s research?

Suggested Writing Assignments

1. Imagine yourself John Henry Sloan (or one of the eight other researchers). Write a personal account of this research on handgun control and your role in it. For an example, see Niko Tinbergen's "The Bee-Hunters of Hulshorst" (NR 953, SE 585).
2. Imagine yourself a journalist whose special area of reporting is science. You read "Handgun Regulations, Crime, Assaults, and Homicide" in the *New England Journal of Medicine* and decide the research is of general interest. Write a news story about it, or editorial, or op-ed piece, or all three.

JACOB BRONOWSKI

The Nature of Scientific Reasoning

The Norton Reader, p. 1008; Shorter Edition, p. 613

"The Nature of Scientific Reasoning" is of a piece with Jacob Bronowski's "The Reach of Imagination" (NR 196, SE 125). In "The Reach of Imagination" he argued that scientific and poetic thinking are essentially the same in that both originate in the imagination. In "The Nature of Scientific Reasoning" he extends his argument to their ends: Scientists and poets search for order, which "must be discovered and, in a deep sense . . . created" (paragraph 9). Central to Bronowski's purposes is disabusing readers of the notion that scientists mechanically accumulate inert facts. Bronowski provides multiple illustrations of scientific discovery ranging from Copernicus to Yukawa and makes them intelligible to nonscientists, that is, if they read them carefully. Students often don't; they skip explanations they expect to be hard to follow or drift away from the text. Making sure they understand Bronowski's examples can be a useful demonstration of active reading: what they have to do to make sense of them, what they have to bring to them, and what strategies, like imaging, are useful.

Analytical Considerations

1. You might have students list Bronowski's illustrations and references, perhaps in two columns labeled science and literature. Which illustrations does he explain, which simply refer to? What do his illustrations and references suggest about his intended audience?
2. Ask the students to list the dates for Bronowski's scientific illustrations. Bronowski turns more extensively to early modern than to modern science, and the example of Yukawa's calculations is less detailed than earlier examples. What does this suggest about modern science? You might refer students to Thomas S. Kuhn's "The Route to Normal Science" (NR 1033, SE 638): in it Kuhn discusses how and when research reports ceased to be intelligible to laypersons (paragraph 17).

Suggested Writing Assignments

1. Write an essay in which you consider the science courses you have taken with respect to Bronowski's assertion, "No scientific theory is a collection of facts" (paragraph 7). Were you taught science in such a way as to make Bronowski's assertion visible? Do you think you should have been?
2. Do library research on current debates over the teaching of science or conduct interviews with science faculty at your institution. What complaints are made about it, what remedies suggested? Write an essay in which you discuss these debates. You may want to use Bronowski's essay to provide a focus for your own.

3. "Science finds order and meaning in our experience" (paragraph 11). Can it be broadened to: "All fields of study find order and meaning in our experience." Write an essay in which you consider a course or courses you have taken in another field of study. Use *I* in a way that seems appropriate to you. How much of your experience will go into your essay, and how will you include it?

Additional questions on this essay will be found in the text (NR 1012, SE 616–17).

STEPHEN JAY GOULD

Darwin's Middle Road

The Norton Reader, p. 1013; Shorter Edition, p. 617

Stephen Jay Gould is a biologist, an historian of science, and a superb popularizer; this essay, like others, was first published in the column he writes for *Natural History* magazine. In "Darwin's Middle Road" he introduces a description of Darwin's working toward natural selection by discussing two opposed views of scientific creativity: inductivism, or reliance on observation and the accumulation of data, and eurekaism, or reliance on predictive hunches and synthesis. Today, he observes, eurakaism is privileged; in Darwin's time, inductivism was. There has been, to use Thomas S. Kuhn's nomenclature, a paradigm shift in accounting for scientific discovery; see "The Route to Normal Science" (NR 1033, SE 630).

Gould, by putting this general discussion first, is better able to present the particulars of Darwin's achievement and we are better able to follow them and his disentangling them from Darwin's own account. Arguing that Darwin shuttled between induction and prediction, Gould puts one piece of evidence after another in place. The structure of his essay, students might be asked to notice, is predictive rather than inductive. Darwin's thinking and Gould's writing may together lead to a useful discussion of the writing process and the relation of rhetoric to thought. Like Darwin, we shuttle between induction and prediction when we think and frequently use our first and intermediate drafts to clarify what we are doing. Final drafts, however, require prediction: The information we present must be shaped to be intelligible to readers.

Analytical Considerations

1. You might ask students to read or review one or more of the following essays in this section: Horace Freeland Judson's "The Rage to Know" (NR 942, SE 574), Niko Tinbergen's "The Bee-Hunters of Hulshorst" (NR 953, SE 585), Jacob Bronowski's "The Nature of Scientific Reasoning" (NR 1008, SE 613), and Thomas S. Kuhn's "The Route to Normal Science" (NR 1033, SE 638). How does each, describing scientific discovery, present what Gould calls inductivism and eurekaism?

2. Gould, at least on the basis of two essays in this section of *The Norton Reader,* is critical of oppositional taxonomies. Ask students to read or review "Scientific Error" (NR 1030, SE 634) and consider as analogous his preferred taxonomies of error and fraud, inductivism and eurekaism.

3. You might ask students to describe their experience of thinking and writing as they produced a recent essay. Does Gould's account of inductivism and prediction clarify the experience for them? This task is best done in groups.

Suggested Writing Assignments

1. Write an essay about a eureka experience of your own. You might consider, in conjunction with it, Gould's conclusion to "Darwin's Middle Road": He quotes Louis Pasteur to the effect that fortune favors the prepared mind.

2. Look at the prescribed form of scientific reporting—abstract, methods, results, discussion, and references—as exemplified by John Henry Sloan et al., "Handgun Regulations, Crime, Assault, and Homicide: A Tale of Two Cities" (NR 966, SE 598). Write an essay in which you consider the relation of its rhetoric to its thought: Is its rhetoric primarily inductive or predictive?

EVELYN FOX KELLER

Women in Science: A Social Analysis

The Norton Reader, p. 1020; Shorter Edition, p. 625

Evelyn Fox Keller, who earned a Ph.D. in physics, now holds a shared appointment in Rhetoric, Women's Studies, and History of Science at the University of California at Berkeley; she has done what she says women in science often do, that is, redefine their field and remove themselves from the mainstream to the periphery of science. This essay surveys subjects she has written about elsewhere: the representation of women in science, childrearing, education, the practice of science, and its methods and goals. She includes autobiographical material, not only about her life but also about the genesis of her inquiry; because she felt a need to assess her own experience and see if it could be generalized, differences between women's and men's minds—or the mythology of differences—seemed an important question.

Fox Keller assumes the situation of women in science is a problem, for men as well as for women. She proposes comprehensive, even revolutionary measures to alleviate it: less-rigid gender stereotyping (entailing massive social reorganization) and encouraging and including women in science (entailing substantial reorganization of scientific practice). Nevertheless, she underplays their revolutionary nature by proposing them persuasively, not as required by justice for women but rather as advantageous to men. Men as well as women, she argues, suffer from the mythology of different intelligences; moreover, scientific thinking at its best is probably androgynous, that is, incorporating and valuing both masculine and feminine qualities (paragraph 24).

Analytical Considerations

1. You might want to ask students to notice the carefully articulated structure of "Women in Science" and compare it with the structure of a scientific report; see John Henry Sloan et al., "Handgun Regulations, Crime, Assaults, and Homicide: A Tale of Two Cities" (NR 966, SE 598). Are there resemblances?
2. You might also want students to notice how the personal figures in this essay; it is possible to adopt the structure of a scientific report without suppressing agents. Nevertheless, Fox Keller does on

occasion write agentless prose: see "Even though it has become fashionable to view such differences as environmental in origin, the temptation to seek ... " (paragraph 1).

3. Fox Keller presents two tables, one of the percentage of Ph.D.'s earned by women from 1920 to 1970 in four fields, another of their representation by rank in the same four fields at twenty leading universities. How does she interpret these tables? Are there additional interpretations to be made? What are the differences by field? What do students think they signify? Why do they think Fox Keller chose these four fields to present? (And have they "read" the tables or skipped them?)

Suggested Writing Assignments

1. Write an essay contextualizing something in your own experience by using a statistical analysis of the phenomenon. Some possibilities: grades, family composition, income, racial and/or ethnic origins, and gender.

2. Write an essay describing elements of your experience of science that raise questions of gender and analyze them. You might consider your experience of science in comparison with your experience of another field of study. Is science more gender marked?

3. Fox Keller says of her own experience as a graduate student that it was "extreme, but possibly illustrative" (paragraph 16). "Women in Science" summarizes it; "The Anomaly of a Woman in Physics," an autobiographical essay written for *Working It Out* (1977), describes it with particularity and feeling. Write an essay in which you consider the relation of "The Anomaly of a Woman in Physics" to "Women in Science."

4. Fox Keller has written a biography of Nobel Prize winner Barbara McClintock, *A Feeling for the Organism* (1983). Read it and use material from it to amplify her remarks, in "Women in Science," on the importance of "fertility and receptivity" to creative science.

Additional questions on this essay will be found in the text (NR 1029, SE 634).

STEPHEN JAY GOULD

Scientific Error

The Norton Reader, p. 1030; Shorter Edition, p. 634

Stephen Jay Gould is a biologist, an historian of science, and a superb popularizer; this essay was published in the *New York Times* in July 1989. The *cause célèbre* of the Baltimore report is explained briefly in footnote 3. In the spring of 1991, David Baltimore, listed as the principal author of six, backed away from defending the senior scientist, Thereza Imanishi-Kari, and there may have been further developments since *The Norton Reader* and the *Guide* went to press. Gould's essay, however, stands somewhat apart from the controversy that prompted it. He enlarges the controversy to consider differences between scientific error and scientific fraud, particularly with respect to scientists' intentions.

Baltimore, a Nobel Prize winner, was head of the Whitehead Institute for Biomedical Research at the Massachusetts Institute of Technology; he is now president of Rockefeller University. The report in question was published in *Cell*, a biomedical journal. The controversy began in 1986, when a postdoctoral fellow, Margot O'Toole, challenged the data reported by Imanishi-Kari. Because other scientists were slow to investigate her charges or to acknowledge error, scientists from the National Institutes of Health (NIH) intervened; an NIH panel found error but not fraud.

Science, particularly science that is intellectually daring, involves, Gould points out, the risk of error. However, he makes this point in a still larger context, the importance of taxonomy, "or the study of classification" (paragraph 8). It makes a difference to our understanding of error and fraud whether we oppose them or set them at the ends of a continuum on which we also place, to use Gould's terms, "serious carelessness," "precipitous grandstanding prompted by the allure of fame or fortune," "finagling," "coverup," and "sloppiness." Because definitions are in part relational, we define error and fraud differently in each instance.

Analytical Considerations

1. For additional information about the Baltimore case at the time Gould wrote "Scientific Error," you might go to Philip Weiss, "Conduct Unbecoming?" (*New York Times Magazine*, October 29,

1989). Weiss raises issues that Gould ignores: scientists' reluctance to police themselves by investigating or acknowledging errors and the closed community of scientists that repudiated the postdoctoral student who discovered them.

2. Taxonomies "embody our most fundamental ideas about the causes of natural order" (paragraph 8). You might ask students to discuss the controversy between Dingell and Baltimore—or between Dingell and Gould—as a controversy about taxonomies. How do they variously define error and fraud, and why do their definitions matter?

3. You might want students to look at the analogies in "Scientific Error," drawn from a range of experience, symphonies to baseball. Some of them work better than others. How are they the sign of a popularizer?

Suggested Writing Assignments

1. Error, Gould concludes his essay, "belongs in the category of proper procedure—for three major reasons": (1) because we are fallible and prone to error; (2) because the more significant the work, the greater the likelihood of error; and (3) because error leads to correction. Locate examples of one or more of Gould's reasons in your own work or in the work of some thinker you have encountered. Write an essay in which you consider the role of error. Are there other legitimate reasons for error that you would add to Gould's?

2. Do library research on the current state of the Baltimore controversy and write a report on it. Would the controversy be easier to resolve if those involved agreed to apply Gould's definitions to it?

3. Do library research on another instance where error or fraud was at stake. You might look at an older instance such as the Piltdown Man, or a more recent instance such as cold fusion. On the basis of the evidence available to you, write an account of it with particular attention to discriminating between error and fraud.

THOMAS S. KUHN

The Route to Normal Science

The Norton Reader, p. 1033; Shorter Edition, p. 638

Thomas S. Kuhn is a Ph.D. in physics turned historian and philosopher of science; "The Route to Normal Science" comes from his best-known work, *The Structure of Scientific Revolutions.* His concept of a paradigm (or a tradition) a paradigm shift (or the end of one research tradition and the beginning of another) has been widely adopted, which is evidence of his influence. For example, we speak of changes in the teaching of writing as a paradigm shift, from emphasizing product (or the finished essay) to process (or its production through multiple drafts).

You might begin class discussion of "The Route to Normal Science" by directing students to its first two paragraphs, in which Kuhn briefly and magisterially lays out the concepts he will illustrate: normal science, the reporting of scientific achievements, the nature of a research tradition, and its relation to scientific practice. Kuhn naturally illustrates these concepts with examples drawn from science. You may be able to enlist knowledgeable students to explain current paradigms; they will probably not be able to explain discarded ones— which in itself illustrates their disappearance. To illustrate a current paradigm, you may want to look at Kuhn's distinction between a textbook and a research report: The references in John Henry Sloan et al.'s "Handgun Regulations, Crime, Assaults, and Homicide: A Tale of Two Cities" (NR 966, SE 598) point to the tradition these researchers built on and extended. To illustrate a discarded paradigm (Kuhn features Newton's optics and Franklin's electricity), Richard S. Westfall's "The Career of Isaac Newton: A Scientific Life in the Seventeenth Century" (NR 995) will help.

Analytical Considerations

1. You might want to look at Kuhn's discussion of paradigms in relation to gathering facts and establishing their relevance (paragraphs 10 and 11). Analogies with writing may be useful here: what gets included and excluded from an essay, when, and why?
2. Kuhn speaks of "the unfortunate simplification that tags an extended historical episode with a single and somewhat arbitrarily chosen name" (paragraph 9). You might ask for examples from history and

literature and consider the various ways they function. Is simplification always "unfortunate"?

Suggested Writing Assignments

1. If you have encountered the term *paradigm* in another field of study, write an essay in which you describe what it refers to and how it is used and discuss whether it is used in Kuhn's sense.
2. Kuhn, in "The Route to Normal Science," mentions what happens to scientists who cling to discarded paradigms (paragraph 15). Elsewhere in *The Structure of Scientific Revolutions* he discusses several of them, including Louis Agassiz, who held out against Darwin. Do library research on Agassiz or another holdout and write a essay about him or her using Kuhn's concept of a paradigm.
3. Kuhn's *The Structure of Scientific Revolutions,* published in 1962, engendered considerable debate that was essentially about definitions. Read his postscript to the second edition (1970) and describe the issues of definition he raises.

Additional questions on this essay will be found in the text (NR 1042, SE 647).

LITERATURE AND THE ARTS

EUDORA WELTY

One Writer's Beginnings

The Norton Reader, p. 1043; Shorter Edition, p. 648

Taken from her best-selling memoir by the same title, this essay returns to the world of Eudora Welty's childhood in Jackson, Mississippi, and offers an adult's reflections on formative early experience. "One Writer's Beginnings" is clearly a chapter from the autobiography of an artist and intellectual. Welty describes the books read to her and the books she read, notes the texts she admired and adored, and talks about the reading process as she experienced it—and as she hopes her readers will also experience it. Perhaps the most important aspect of "One Writer's Beginnings" comes near the end when Welty considers "voice." Her six-paragraph treatment of the subject, beginning with her mother's songs and records played on the Victrola, then retracing her own reading and writing experience, provides a valuable opportunity to define and illustrate this difficult rhetorical concept.

Analytical Considerations

1. Why does Welty devote so much space to describing the books of her childhood? Are they the forces that most powerfully shaped her, or is she, through memory and words, also (re)shaping the self she presents in this autobiography of an artist?
2. Ask students why this selection has been titled "One Writer's Beginnings." Would they expect different "beginnings" from the autobiography of, say, a painter or politician or businessperson?
3. Welty says, "Movement must be at the very heart of listening" (paragraph 22). This principle is also true for reading. Ask students to plot the movement of "One Writer's Beginnings" and then to consider what unifies the piece.
4. In what ways is Welty's essay a cultural document reflecting the world of the American South in the early decades of this century? You might begin discussion of this question by asking students to note what is different about Welty's childhood from their own—or, perhaps, what details from Welty's childhood they have

encountered in stories told by their parents or grandparents.

5. Welty obviously loves books and loves to talk about them. Ask students what strategies she uses to communicate her responses—not just adjectives, but metaphors, memories, anecdotes—and what strategies most excited them, as readers, about the pleasures of books.

6. Ask students to respond to Welty's discussion of her "physical awareness of the word." Have they had similar experiences? About what words?

7. In paragraph 24 Welty offers a fine description of "voice" in a story or poem. After discussing it, ask students to characterize the voice they hear in "One Writer's Beginnings."

Suggested Writing Assignments

1. In describing her reading of classic tales from *Every Child's Story Book*, Welty notes: "I located myself in these pages and could go straight to the stories and pictures I loved" (paragraph 11). If you have had a similar experience with stories or books, write an essay about it. If your experience with books was quite different, that, too, might provide the subject of an essay.

2. Welty lists many of the children's tales she read and loved as she grew up. If you have read any of these tales, reread it again and, in an analytical essay, suggest why it continues to appeal to children.

3. "Learning stamps you with its moments. Childhood's learning is made up of moments. It isn't steady. It's a pulse" (paragraph 15). Reflect on your own educational process, both formal and informal; then write an essay in response to Welty's observation about how learning occurs.

4. Turn your response to Analytical Consideration 6—about "physical awareness of the word"—into an essay on "The Vision of the Artist."

Additional questions on this essay will be found in the text (NR 1049, SE 654).

VLADIMIR NABOKOV

Good Readers and Good Writers

The Norton Reader, p. 1050; Shorter Edition, p. 655

Although Nabokov is well-known to teachers of literature and writing, his work may be unfamiliar to the students in our classes. In preparation for this and Alice Munro's "What is Real?" (NR 1071, SE 660), about reading and writing fiction, you may want your students to read a short story by one or both of these writers and to think about how the writers' essays reflect their fictional preferences.

More generally, you may want to ask students what they expect from fiction: Why they read, what please them, what satisfies them at a story's end. Nabokov's views on what "good" readers ought to expect may prove quite different from theirs; indeed, through the imaginary "quiz" he gives, Nabokov insists that action, emotional identification, and historical interest are not "good" motives for reading. Rather than treat his ideas as authoritative, it may be more effective to present them as one writer's plea for how he wants his work to be read.

Analytical Considerations

1. Why does Nabokov use a quotation from the French novelist Flaubert in the opening paragraph of his essay? What does the quotation tell us about the style, tone, and persona of the writer?
2. In paragraph 5, Nabokov gives a "quiz" about "good" readers—which he claims he once gave to students. Why does he give this quiz rather than present his ideas more directly? Does he, in a sense, coerce us as readers into choosing the right answers?
3. What are the two varieties of imagination that Nabokov describes? Try to summarize the difference between the two in a sentence.
4. At the end of the essay, Nabokov retells the story of the boy who cried wolf (paragraph 11). What is the standard version of this story? Why does Nabokov revise it? What new meaning does he want us to grasp?
5. Nabokov writes that a writer is at least three things: storyteller, teacher, and entertainer. Which of these three dominates in this essay?
6. The essay ends with an image: the artist who "build[s] his castle of cards," which turns into "a castle of beautiful steel and glass." Ask students to analyze this image, what sense of the artist it conveys,

and why Nabokov chooses to end with it.

Suggested Writing Assignments

1. Write an argument for or against Nabokov's suggestion that "the good reader is one who has imagination, memory, a dictionary, and some artistic sense" (paragraph 5) rather than an inclination toward "emotional identification, action, and the socio-economic or historical angle."
2. Read a story written by Vladimir Nabokov and suggest the ways in which his fiction reflects the value stated in "Good Readers and Good Writers."
3. Compare and contrast the views of Nabokov and Munro on what is "real" and what is "fiction." On what points do they agree? On what might they disagree?

ALICE MUNRO

What Is Real?

The Norton Reader, p. 1071; Shorter Edition, p. 660

Alice Munro's essay, a revised version of a public talk, addresses an issue many readers wonder about: To what extent is a writer's fiction based on her own life's experiences? As Munro notes, this issue bothers the people of Wingham, Ontario, where she grew up. Because she sometimes uses "real" details from town history, readers assume that Wingham is "like" the narrow, unpleasant towns in Munro's fiction—an assumption that Winghamites resent. They have criticized Munro for making them the "butt of a soured and cruel introspection" (paragraph 4).

In preparation for discussion of "What Is Real?" you might ask students what they assume to be the relation of a writer's life and fiction. If you teach in a town or city that has produced a great writer, you might even ask students to read a biography or visit a local museum to see what sort of relation is commonly assumed. In any case, this essay—perhaps in conjunction with a piece of writing like Maxine Hong Kingston's "Tongue-Tied" (NR 381, SE 230)— can provoke a more sophisticated approach to the terms *truth* and *fiction*.

Analytical Considerations

1. Munro's "What Is Real?" originated as a public talk. What verbal clues give this origin away? How does the occasion influence Munro's style?
2. If your class read Vladimir Nabokov's "Good Readers and Good Writers" (NR 1050, SE 655), you might ask students to compare the styles of the two writers (which are quite different, despite the similar origins of their essays). What impression does each writer (seek to) create?
3. In the course of her essay, Munro uses various metaphors for writing fiction—for example building a house (paragraphs 8 and 9) or using "a bit of starter dough" (paragraph 11). Discuss the way such metaphors function as explanations for the process of writing.
4. The final paragraph contains Munro's "answer" to the question her essay raises. In what sense is it an answer? Why does she delay her answer until this point?

Suggested Writing Assignments

1. Read one of Alice Munro's short stories (from *Lives of Girls and Women*, for example), and try to address these questions: Why do Munro's people and places seem "real"? What features of Munro's writing contribute to this conflation of the real and the fictional? What do we, as readers, lose if we approach the story as "autobiographical" versus "fictional"?
2. Munro compares a short story to a house, something that "encloses space and makes connections between one enclosed space and another" (paragraph 7). Does this metaphor apply to the structure of "What Is Real?" If so, write an analysis in which you describe Munro's essay in terms of its rooms, passages, and other architectural features.
3. See Suggested Writing Assignment 3 for Vladimir Nabokov, "Good Readers and Good Writers" (G 174).

NORTHROP FRYE

The Motive for Metaphor

The Norton Reader, p. 1055; Shorter Edition, p. 663

In this essay, part of a series of talks for students and critics of
literature, Northrop Frye develops a theory of creative language and an
apologia for literature. His own use of metaphor and analogy makes
this a form of metareflection. Frye's ability to pose resonant questions
(in regard to the social value of literature, the identity of the poet, the
differences between art and science) and to suggest possible responses
distinguishes this essay from others like it, which find the roots of
imagination in our human desires and mental capacities.

Analytical Considerations

1. What is the "motive for metaphor"? You might approach this
   question either by asking students what, according to Frye,
   metaphor achieves or by discussing the quotation from Wallace
   Stevens at the end of Frye's essay.
2. What are the three levels of the mind? How does each operate? Why
   does Frye take such pains to distinguish them?
3. In paragraphs 5, 12, and 13 Frye presents his understanding of how
   science works. Compare and contrast that with the understanding of
   Jacob Bronowski in "The Nature of Scientific Reasoning" (NR
   1008, SE 613) or Stephen Jay Gould in "Darwin's Middle Road"
   (NR 1013, SE 617).
4. How does Frye distinguish the arts from the sciences? Ask students
   whether they see any limitations in his distinctions.
5. Why does Frye devote a substantial paragraph to his understanding
   that "literature doesn't evolve or improve or progress" (paragraph
   13)?
6. Why does Frye pose the following question: "Is it possible that
   literature, especially poetry, is something that a scientific
   civilization like ours will eventually outgrow" (paragraph 14)?
   What response does he expect us to have?
7. Important to this essay is the extended analogy of shipwrecked
   existence. In the last paragraph, Frye notes that "analogy, or
   likeness to something else, is very tricky to handle in description,
   because the differences are as important as the resemblances." Has
   Frye himself succeeded or failed here?

8. How does Frye use questions, particularly in the opening paragraph? Where else does he use them? How and why? Compare and contrast his use with that of Bronowski in "The Nature of Scientific Reasoning."
9. Have students plot the design of this essay, accounting for organization, development, direction, and points of emphasis. The concluding paragraph merits special consideration.

Suggested Writing Assignments

1. Write an essay illustrating Frye's assertion that "the simplest questions are not only the hardest to answer, but the most important to ask" (paragraph 1).
2. Write an essay comparing and contrasting Frye and Bronowski ("The Reach of Imagination") on the function of the imagination.

Additional questions on this essay will be found in the text (NR 1063–64, SE 671–72).

ANNIE DILLARD

About Symbol

The Norton Reader, p. 1064; Shorter Edition, p. 672

Like Northrop Frye's "A Motive for Metaphor" (NR 1055, SE 663) and Robert Frost's "Education by Poetry: A Meditative Monologue" (NR 1091, SE 680), Annie Dillard's "About Symbol" takes up the question of the function and value of the "literary." Like Frye, Dillard distinguishes between the knowledge of science and the knowledge of art—and you might want to ask your students why writers and literary critics seem so concerned to demonstrate the value of art. (If your students feel pressure from their families to choose a practical major, like engineering or biology, rather than a major like English or art history, you will have a ready-made example of how modern society acknowledges the importance of the scientific and questions the value of the artistic.) Dillard finds that value in the symbolic imagination and in art as a "cognitive instrument." What Frye associates with metaphor, she discusses in terms of symbol.

Analytical Considerations

1. Why does Dillard begin by questioning the relative values of art versus science? How does she distinguish between the provinces of each? If you have read Northrop Frye's "A Motive for Metaphor," you might compare their answers and their modes of analysis.

2. In paragraph 3, Dillard describes art as "a material mock-up of bright idea." What does she mean? Why does she use this formulation?

3. How does Dillard distinguish between "allegorical symbol" and "nonallegorical symbol"? Which does she imply is superior? To help students answer this question, you might want to unravel the sentence in paragraph 6 beginning, "When fair-haired Virtue shatters the opium pipe of Indolence," as a way of showing students how Dillard illustrates her point even as she makes it.

4. In paragraph 2 Dillard offers a series of sentences describing the juncture of science and theology, and again in paragraph 10 she offers a series describing the artistic symbol. Both use the sentence form "It is . . . ." You might ask students to explain one of these series—both its meaning and its rhetorical function.

5. Students may find the extended reference to Coleridge's "Kubla Khan" difficult, if not exclusionary. The poem is reprinted in *The Norton Reader* so that classes can discuss it as well as Dillard's essay. But you may want to ask your students more generally why Dillard chooses this poem: How does it embody her ideas about symbol?

Suggested Writing Assignments

1. Write an essay in which you explain the function and value of literature versus that of science. Draw on the ideas of Frye and Dillard if you wish, but formulate the essay in your own terms.

2. Analyze a symbol familiar to you from religion, government, or education in terms of Dillard's concepts of how symbols function.

Additional questions on this essay will be found in the text (NR 1068–71, SE 676–79).

ROBERT FROST

Education by Poetry: A Meditative Monologue

The Norton Reader, p. 1091; Shorter Edition, p. 680

Robert Frost's personal and rather quirky address to Amherst students in 1930 will acquaint students with one of twentieth-century America's most famous writers, whose poetry they may have sampled but who looms as a literary figure rather than as a distinct personality. "Education by Poetry" should remedy that, for here Frost reveals much about himself not only by what he says but by how he says it. The poet presents himself as a teacher and, in the course of developing his thoughts on poetic metaphor, interjects his views on the role of colleges in imparting "taste and judgment." Frost believes that college students should learn the ability to discern metaphor in the world beyond poetry—in science, philosophy, history, psychology. In a voice both humorous and cantankerous, Frost takes us on a circuitous route to the understanding that poetry teaches metaphor, that metaphor leads to belief—in self, love, country, God—and that belief is the only means of bringing something into being, of living creatively and responsively. By Frost's oddly rambling, oddly unified reasoning, poetry becomes the basis of life.

Analytical Considerations

1. Explain Frost's thesis: "Education by poetry is education by metaphor" (paragraph 9). Ask students to clarify the ways in which Frost understands metaphor.
2. What does Frost mean when he says, "To learn to write is to learn to have ideas" (paragraph 37)? You might connect his statement with current ideas about writing as a mode of discovery.
3. Why does Frost not offer his reader examples of the metaphors "to live by"?
4. Why does Frost explore the several dimensions of the word *belief*?
5. In what ways do Frost and Northrop Frye in "The Motive for Metaphor" (NR 1055, SE 663), agree and/or disagree on the meaning and function of metaphor? Does Frost mean by metaphor what Annie Dillard in "About Symbol" (NR 1064, SE 672) identifies as symbol?
6. In perhaps a dozen places Frost digresses or becomes parenthetic. Are these digressions distractions or effective rhetorical devices that

contribute to his purpose?

7. Ask students to determine if there is order or a pattern to this essay. If so, what provides the thread of continuity? Is it persona? theme? imagery?

8. "Education by Poetry" was originally a speech. How is an oral performance different from a written presentation? If you had the chance to work with Frost and prepare this speech for publication, what changes would you suggest? Why?

Suggested Writing Assignments

1. The Latin poet Horace said that poetry should both delight and teach. Would Frost agree? Does Frost do so in his prose as well as in his poetry? Write a careful, analytical essay on the subject.

2. Write an essay on what poetry and/or poets mean to you.

3. Write an essay in response to Frost's declaration, "We ask people to think, and we don't show them what thinking is" (paragraph 37). Draw examples from your own and other students' experience.

Additional questions on this essay will be found in the text (NR 1099–1100, SE 688–89).

ROBERTSON DAVIES

Ham and Tongue

The Norton Reader, p. 1125; Shorter Edition, p. 689

The Canadian writer Robertson Davies is best known for his fiction and drama, but in "Ham and Tongue" he shows himself to be a superb public speaker as well. "Ham and Tongue" is a speech that illustrates its principles, that articulates what good public speaking is, and that shows by example how to do it. For Davies the basic principles of public speaking fall under two headings: "ham," the mode of presentation, and "tongue," the choice of words.

Because many of the essays in this section originated as public talks, you may want to ask how writers like Vladimir Nabokov, Northrop Frye, Annie Dillard, or Robert Frost would fare if Davies were evaluating their speeches. This approach may produce some negative remarks about the speaking abilities of famous writers, but it can also lead to an important discussion about the limits of speech: What can a writer do in *writing* that a speaker cannot do in *speech*? Alternatively, you may want your students to analyze the speech of a politician or other public figure for the mode of "sincerity" that Davies criticizes or for the features of "ham" and "tongue" he defines.

Analytical Considerations

1. What does Davies mean by "ham" and "tongue"? Where and how does he define the terms?
2. Because "Ham and Tongue" is a speech about the art of public speaking, we might expect Davies to exemplify the principles he praises—and, indeed, he does. Where and how does Davies show us "ham" and "tongue" in action?
3. In a public talk, the speaker must often make his or her major points and transitions more emphatically than a writer does in print, where readers can return to a paragraph if they seem to have missed something. Where and how does Davies underscore his main points? How do his transitions help his readers to hear these points?
4. Ask several students to prepare a paragraph or two from Davies' speech for oral delivery. When were they conscious of "ham" and "tongue" as principles to remember? What other issues arise in oral presentation?
5. "Ham and Tongue" ends with a brief comparison of Marcus Brutus and Mark Antony as public orators. Draw out the implications of this illustration and suggest why Davies ends with it but does not elaborate on it.

Suggested Writing Assignments

1. Rewrite one of the essays in this section as a speech that exemplifies the principles of "Ham and Tongue." If possible, deliver it to the class and comment briefly on the changes that were necessary.
2. Using Davies' criteria for good public speaking, analyze one of the essays in this section that began as a public talk (e.g., those by Nabokov, Frye, Dillard, Frost, or Woolf). What do you think Davies would think about the speech as speech? What other criteria might its writer have had in mind when preparing the speech?

SCOTT RUSSELL SANDERS

The Singular First Person

The Norton Reader, p. 1100; Shorter Edition, p. 696

Scott Russell Sanders' "The Singular First Person" is the only essay in this section specifically about the essay form itself, rather than more generally about the value of literature. Scott locates the personal essay somewhere between pure "autobiography," which dwells "complacently on the self" and which anyone from a mass murderer to a great statesman can publish, and the impersonal scientific or committee report, which more often than not produces "textureless tasteless mush." Since students will have read many other essays before they reach Sanders', you might ask them what they would list as the traits and values of the essay, and then compare their lists with Sanders' main points. You might also ask them which essays and essayists in *The Norton Reader* have been their favorites, and see if their choices coincide with Sanders'.

Analytical Considerations

1. Why effect does Sanders' opening anecdote have on the reader? How does it both convey a common criticism that the essay and essayist are "egocentric" and, simultaneously, lessen the possibility that such criticism might be leveled against Sanders?
2. At what other points in the essay does Sanders anticipate potential criticism and divert it? Ask students to formulate this technique as a rhetorical principle.
3. Early in his essay (paragraph 4), Sanders gives a list of important contemporary essay writers. What is the rhetorical purpose of this list? What other names would you add?
4. Sanders defends the essayist against the fiction writer (and against the possible assumption that fiction is "better" than nonfiction). How does he make this defense?
5. Sanders refers to rules that he was taught in English composition classes—for example, against using the "I" or against using mixed metaphors—and proceeds to break them before our eyes. Ask students to analyze how and why he breaks the rules, but also how he implicitly acknowledges the purpose of the rules (as, for example, when his metaphors get out of control).
6. Sanders devotes a long section to the history of the essay and what

its writers have said of the genre. What is its purpose?

7. Near the end of the essay, Sanders quarrels with literary critics who taught him about the "intentional fallacy" (paragraph 27). Sanders defines that fallacy within his essay, but you may want to explain it more fully to your students. After doing so, ask your students why Sanders disagrees with literary critics—and why a writer like Vladimir Nabokov or Alice Munro might take a different position.

8. The essay ends with a metaphor that captures Sanders' notion of "singularity." Do a close reading of this ending, considering how the final metaphor enriches what Sanders has already said.

Suggested Writing Assignments

1. List three or four features that Sanders considers essential to the essay form. Then analyze one of your favorite essays in terms of these features. Does it exemplify them? Does the essay have other important features that Sanders fails to take note of? You may want to use Sander's own essay "Looking at Women" (NR 222, SE 106).

2. Near the beginning of his essay, Sanders shows us the function—and possible dysfunctions—of metaphorical language when he compares the making of an essay to the "romping of a dog and then to the surge of a river" (paragraph 11). Analyze another essay from this section in which metaphors are abundant, explaining where you find the metaphors effective or, alteratively, where they lead the writer and reader astray.

3. Find the personal essay Sanders refers to near the end of "The First Person Singular," the one that a scholar treated as a piece of fiction. Why did the scholar make this mistake? What features of the essay seemed to signal fiction? What features should have signaled nonfiction? Is it always possible to tell the difference?

Additional questions on this essay will be found in the text (NR 1110, SE 706–07).

VIRGINIA WOOLF

In Search of a Room of One's Own

The Norton Reader, p. 1111; Shorter Edition, p. 707

This essay is Chapter 3 of Virginia Woolf's *A Room of One's Own*, a central document in twentieth-century feminist criticism and scholarship. The work began in 1928 as lectures given to undergraduates at two of Cambridge University's women's colleges, Girton and Newnham. Woolf then developed her lectures into a text. "In Search of a Room of One's Own" presents Woolf at her characteristic best: impassioned, witty, learned, and insightful. The essay operates on the historical, imaginative, and personal levels simultaneously, for Woolf writes about the plight of women writers in history—emblematized by the fictitious Judith Shakespeare—which leads to expression of her own concern that women who would write need to find the means and space to work undistractedly.

Analytical Considerations

1. Ask students what they infer from Woolf's title, "A Room of One's Own."
2. Why does Woolf choose to focus on the living conditions of women in England during the time of Elizabeth I? What rhetorical effect can she achieve by using the age of Shakespeare rather than, say, the age of Pope?
3. Explain what Woolf means when she says that "fiction is like a spider's web, attached ever so lightly perhaps, but still attached to life at all four corners" (paragraph 2). What other images might one use for fiction that would serve Woolf's purpose less well?
4. What, according to Woolf, is the image of womanhood gained from studying poetry and fiction written by men? Do you agree with her assessment?
5. What does Woolf mean by saying, "It is one of the great advantages of being a woman that one can pass even a very fine negress without wishing to make an Englishwoman of her" (paragraph 9)?
6. How does Woolf answer the question she poses: "What is the state of mind that is most propitious to the act of creation" (paragraph 10)?
7. Ask students to focus on the last seven sentences of paragraph 6 (about the bishop), and analyze what each sentence does. What is

the total effect of the passage? How does Woolf use the bishop again? Does he become a metaphor in this essay?

8. In what ways is this a cultural document? In what ways is this a personal statement?

9. Do Frances FitzGerald, in "Rewriting American History" (NR 818, SE 483), and Woolf share similar concerns and strategies?

10. This essay was once a lecture, shaped by the demands and conventions of spoken performance. After discerning the textual clues that characterize the piece as a lecture, turn to other essays by Woolf in *The Norton Reader*, all of them written for publication, not for oral delivery. Ask your students to study them for the ways in which Woolf adapts her techniques and style to an audience of readers rather than listeners. Perhaps even direct the reading and discussion toward the preparation of an essay on this topic.

Suggested Writing Assignments

1. Write an essay in response to Woolf's description of "that very interesting and obscure masculine complex . . . ; that deep-seated desire, not so much that she shall be inferior as that he shall be superior" (paragraph 14).

2. *Unimpeded* is a key word in Woolf's essay. Discuss what the term represents in political, physical, and psychological terms for the artists—men, women, or both—whom Woolf discusses.

3. Write an essay in response to the question: Do women now have a room of their own?

LANCE MORROW

Imprisoning Time in a Rectangle

The Norton Reader, p. 1082; Shorter Edition, p. 718

"Imprisoning Time in a Rectangle" explores the meaning of photography: its function, its power, its dangers, its effects. Originally published in a *Time* magazine special collection, *The Best of Photojournalism,* the essay asks the question: What is photojournalism? Lance Morrow answers that it is "the first impression of history," i.e., it captures the historical moment, but also that it is "history's lasting visual impression," i.e., that it helps to create history.

Because the essay discusses two famous examples of photojournalism that affected history—the image of Jack Ruby shooting Lee Harvey Oswald and the photo of General Loan, police chief of Saigon, shooting a Viet Cong in the temple—you may want to bring these photographs into class. It is worth asking students what they "see" in these images, telling them what you see (particularly if you remember the original appearances), and discussing what Morrow sees. These differences (and coincidences) of vision might lead to an interesting discussion of how we read photographs and how our understanding of history influences our readings.

Analytical Considerations

1. Why does Morrow begin with the story of Balzac's fear, then continue with the image of an onion being peeled, layer by layer? What do story and image have in common? How are they different (and thus supplemental in what they teach us about photography)?
2. How does Morrow define journalism? How does he define photojournalism? Both the notion of "first impression" and "lasting visual impression" are crucial to understanding Morrow's sense that the photograph both reflects and creates historical reality.
3. Analyze one of the photographs Morrow refers to. How does he add to our understanding by explaining the context in which the photograph was taken? What misimpressions are we susceptible to within knowing the contexts?
4. Why does Morrow allude to "the puritan conscience" in the final paragraph? What does he mean by "the ghost of the golden calf"? What danger in photography does he suggest?

Suggested Writing Assignments

1. By browsing through collections of photojournalism in the library, find a photograph of an important historical event—whether from past or recent history—and analyze it. How does that photograph "interpret" history? Is there contextual information that the viewer should know to understand the photograph better?
2. By comparing two newspapers or magazines, find two or more photographs of the same current event. Compare and contrast these two photographs for the way they interpret the event.
3. If you have access to an art museum, study a historical painting for the way it interprets history, using some of the principles Morrow raises in his essay.

Additional questions on this essay will be found in the text (NR 1085, SE 720–21).

AARON COPLAND

How We Listen

The Norton Reader, p. 1133; Shorter Edition, p. 721

Aaron Copland, long one of America's best-loved composers, writes a clear and cogent analysis of the listening process in "How We Listen." In explaining the basic concepts of music appreciation, Copland's essay neatly illustrates the rhetorical mode of classification and the principles of analysis and synthesis. Because of Copland's wish to both inform and instruct, he takes great pains to be clear. The design of his essay, the use of example and analogy, and the simplicity of language and syntax help accomplish his purpose, leading us to the conclusion that we listen to music on several different levels of appreciation at the same time. This essay provides one model of how an expert can communicate ideas at a level and in a form accessible to his audience.

Analytical Considerations

1. Why do we "find Tchaikovsky easier to 'understand' than Beethoven" (paragraph 10)? What criteria is Copland using?
2. Does Copland give us his criteria for determining who is the "greater" composer, Ravel or Beethoven? What are they?
3. Why does Copland oppose attempts to pin "a meaning-word" on music?
4. Ask students to plot the design of this essay, annotating each paragraph to show how it functions within the scheme of the whole.
5. How well does Copland use the mode of classification to develop "How We Listen"? Are his categories mutually exclusive and clearly explained?
6. How does Copland use analogy? Is it effective? Is it essential to his purpose?
7. What are readers to make of Copland's references to "simple-minded souls" and the "man in the street" or "one timid lady"? Do we identity with or also associate ourselves from such references?

How, then, do these labels function as rhetorical devices?

Suggested Writing Assignments

1. The author mentions the "subjective and objective attitude" necessary to musical composition. Write an essay analyzing his three categories of listening as a subjective or objective process.
2. Does Copland make or imply any judgments that would indicate that he considers one "plane" of appreciation more worthwhile than the others? Explain.
3. Write a rhetorical analysis of "How We Listen," carefully detailing the means by which Copland succeeds or fails in discussing a difficult topic.
4. Apply the categories of listening discussed in Copland's essay to a piece of his own music. Consider a piece that has a theme.

PHILOSOPHY AND RELIGION

LANGSTON HUGHES

Salvation

The Norton Reader, p. 1196; Shorter Edition, p. 727

"Salvation" reveals in full measure Langston Hughes' gifts as a storyteller: economy and precision of language a keen car for dialogue a sharp eye for descriptive detail a detached ironic voice a capacity for seriousness with humor. Hughes' re-creation of a revival meeting, set in rural America around 1914 or 1915, is a cultural document—an expose of the sometimes dishonest theatrics of a manipulative preacher in front of a gullible flock of souls. It is also an account of an experience of considerable symbolic importance in Hughes' memory; as such it might be considered a rite of passage narrative.

Analytical Considerations

1. How do we know that "Salvation" was written by an adult? Why did Hughes write it? You might lead students to an understanding of autobiography as both record and reflection, personal experience with cultural resonance.
2. What is the tone of Hughes' first sentence? Of his second sentence? What is the effect of paragraph 12, which consists of one four-word sentence?
3. Ask students to analyze Hughes' technique as a narrator. Is his narrative effective? Why or why not?
4. Compare and contrast Hughes' ability to recapture childhood experience with that of Dylan Thomas, Maya Angelou, or Annie Dillard.
5. Why does Hughes title his account "Salvation"? Who is being saved—and from what?

Suggested Writing Assignments

1. Write a personal essay in which you recount feeling pressured into doing something you would have preferred to avoid. Try to convey, as Hughes does, both your feelings at the time and your present attitude toward the experience.

2. Write an essay on the ways in which "Salvation" re-creates a particular time and place. Do you think, for example, it is important that some characters are named but that no specific location is cited?
3. Write an essay on "Salvation" as a rite of passage narrative, discussing how Hughes' experience at the revival meeting changed his perception. Or write your own rite-of-passage narrative.

Additional questions on this essay will be found in the text (NR 1198, SE 729).

ROBERT GRAVES

Mythology

The Norton Reader, p. 1177; Shorter Edition, p. 729

Robert Graves' "Mythology" looks at religious beliefs from a scientific or anthropological perspective—that is, from the perspective of nonbelief. Graves defines what myth is and how it functions, particularly as a means of explanation and of justification for social and political systems. Originally written as an encyclopedia entry, for the *Larousse Encyclopedia of World Mythology*, you might want your students to compare it with other such entries to see how artful Graves' writing can be. You might also want to refer them to Graves' classic study of mythology, *The White Goddess*.

Analytical Considerations

1. How does Graves define mythology? After discussing his definition, ask students how he would define religion.
2. Graves suggests that myth has two main functions. What are they? Why does he define them both briefly at the beginning of his essay, before giving extended illustrations?
3. The bulk of Graves' essay, paragraphs 5 through 11, illustrates the two functions of myth. How is this section organized?
4. As he illustrates myths used to justify existing social systems, Graves explains how the takeover of matriarchal systems by patriarchal ones is reflected in changing myths. You might ask students whether Graves implies that myths merely reflect social change or whether myths might actually help to bring about change.

Is it possible to change social and political systems today by changing our myths?

Suggested Writing Assignments

1. Choose one of the deities described in "Mythology," consult several reference books to learn more about its origin and cultural function, and write a brief account summarizing what you have learned.
2. Graves does not discuss Jewish or Christian stories as if they were myths. How might he have done so? Use one particular biblical story to illustrate your application of Graves' method.

PLATO

The Allegory of the Cave

The Norton Reader, p. 1153; Shorter Edition, p. 734

"The Allegory of the Cave" comes from Plato's great treatise on politics and government, the *Republic*. In it Plato, using his teacher Socrates as his mouthpiece, instructs Glaucon on the subject of human knowledge. Chained in an underground den, the cave dwellers see only their shadows on the wall, cast by the fire behind them. The shadows, which suggest the pure forms that exist in the realm of ideas, constitute the reality of the cave dwellers. By training the mind to contemplate the pure forms, the cave dwellers can struggle into the sunlit world of ideas above.

Plato's use of the literary form of allegory and his characteristic use of the Socratic dialogue may require some explanation and discussion. You might consider doing a rhetorical unit on allegory, working with allegorical writing by Aesop in "The Frogs Desiring a King" (NR 1153), James Thurber in "The Owl Who Was God" (NR 1176), and George Orwell. The allegorical tradition presents opportunities to consider reading as a process for creating meaning at an accessible level.

Analytical Considerations

1. What is Socrates trying to teach Glaucon in "The Allegory of the Cave"? Is it a lesson about abstract qualities?
2. Plato's allegory may be read as a discussion of appearance and

reality; as such, it deals with long-standing polarities between the two. Why are human beings so distrustful of appearances?

3. Are there people who "entertain these false notions and live in this miserable manner" (paragraph 28) today?
4. Ask students whether they accept the conclusion set forth in the last line—and why.
5. Socrates offers his own interpretation of the allegory, but it is one among a number of others. What is it meant to represent? What does it represent? How do we know?
6. Ask students to comment on the imagery of sight and light and how it functions. Are these clusters stylistic devices? Do they have metaphoric importance?
7. Ask students to describe the features of a Socratic dialogue. What is the role of "instructor"? the student? Do they think it is an effective means of teaching?
8. Does this allegory, now more than twenty-five centuries old, have relevance to readers today?

Suggested Writing Assignments

1. Because meaning emerges only when you read—Mand often write about—a text, write an essay in which you interpret "The Allegory of the Cave" by offering a reading of your own.
2. Write an essay setting forth the advantages and disadvantages of applying the Socratic method to undergraduate education today.
3. Do some research on Plato and Socrates. Then write a 750-word essay that might serve as an introduction to "The Allegory of the Cave" in *The Norton Reader*.

VIRGINIA WOOLF

The Death of the Moth

The Norton Reader, p. 1214; Shorter Edition, p. 738

This essay, one of Virginia Woolf's best-known works of nonfiction, combines narration and description in the service of definition. Woolf writes with feeling but not sentiment, offering her reader a carefully realized observation before speculating about the meaning of that observation.

Woolf plays the role of observer and reporter in this essay. What begins as idle curiosity becomes conscious speculation, but no explicit conclusions are drawn. Although she points to possible meaning immanent in the death throes of the moth, she does not overshadow the event itself with ponderous philosophical analysis. Her technique here might be contrasted with that of other essayists who draw out their meanings more directly; students might be asked to think about how the writer's choices interact with discourse conventions to create the range of possibilities in the essay form.

Analytical Considerations

1. Ask students what aspects of "The Death of the Moth" they remember best-and why? Imagery will likely be relevant to their responses. If so, have students select several images and describe the primary appeal of each (visual, aural, tactile). Then ask them to determine how each image functions within the essay.
2. Does Woolf offer a thesis statement? Does she have a central point she wishes to make, or is her essay a speculative exercise, more important for the writing than the content?
3. You might want students to describe the persona Woolf has created here. How does she create it? Is her use of the third person ("one") in much of the essay important in this regard? Why does she shift to the first person in the last paragraphs? How does her language suggest detachment as well as emotional involvement or impact?
4. How and to what effect has Woolf used a kind of triple focus (the world "out there", the moth, and the narrator) in this essay?
5. What is the relationship between the life and death of the moth and the life and death of human beings in "The Death of the Moth"? Does Woolf offer any conclusions about death in this piece?
6. Compare Woolf's style and persona in this selection to that in "My Father: Leslie Stephen" (NR 134, SE 70).

Suggested Writing Assignments

1. If the death of an animal has moved you to speculate on significant questions concerning life and death, write an essay describing and analyzing the experience.
2. With ironic understatement, Woolf writes, "The insignificant little creature now knew death" (paragraph 5). Yet this little creature was not insignificant. Write an essay explaining why.

Additional questions on this essay will be found in the text (NR 1216–17, SE 740–41).

GILBERT HIGHET

The Mystery of Zen

The Norton Reader, p. 1205; Shorter Edition, p. 741

In "The Mystery of Zen," Gilbert Highet, a distinguished teacher and author of *The Art of Teaching*, writes about a German philosopher, Eugen Herrigel, who studied under a Zen master for six years. Highet is at least as concerned with the method by which Herrigel learned as with the content of what he learned from his lengthy course in Zen archery. At a deeper and somewhat more abstract level, the essay confronts the difficulties of describing the mystical dimension of human existence, which, Highet concludes, cannot be analyzed but must be lived to be understood.

Analytical Considerations

1. What is the "mystery of Zen"? Does Highet convey the mystery successfully?
2. What does "Zen meditation" mean to Highet? What techniques does he use to present his understanding?
3. How does Highet distinguish "philosophical teachers" from "mystical writers"?
4. Ask students if they feel satisfied with the way Highet defines "meditation" in paragraph 15. Can it be "a way of life" in twentieth-century Western society?
5. Highet's discussion of mystical writers (paragraph 18) is worth considering in detail, for he dwells on the insufficiency of language "to describe experiences which are too abstruse for words." In what situations and in what ways does language fail us? Why do we "fall back on imagery and analogy"? If you have read Annie Dillard's "About Symbol" (NR 1064, SE 672),you might ask students whether Highet and Dillard are confronting the same problem and finding the same answers.
6. By the end of the essay, do you accept Highet's assertion that "Zen is a religion rather than a philosophy"? Why or why not?
7. Highet obviously appreciates and admires the Zen philosophy or practice. How does he convey his attitude?

Suggested Writing Assignments

1. Highet's introduction to "The Mystery of Zen" suggests that one can get new meaning from books (or essays, or poems, or paintings, perhaps) that one returns to after some absence. Have you had any experience of this sort? Describe it in an essay.
2. Consider "The Mystery of Zen" as an essay on the art of teaching. Write an essay, "Zen and the Art of _____," in which you detail the techniques of Zen instruction as they apply to an interest of yours.

Additional questions on this essay will be found in the text (NR 1213–14, SE 750).

JEAN-PAUL SARTRE

Existentialism

The Norton Reader, p. 1229; Shorter Edition, p. 750

Existentialism is perhaps the most significant philosophy to be propounded in recent history, and this essay presents one of the most coherent statements we have of the existentialist position. Jean-Paul Sartre anchors his discussion to the famous existentialist catchphrase "existence precedes essence" (paragraph 3). What he develops, then, in the essay are the implications of this assertion. The phrase suggests, generally, that man is responsible for what he is and what he becomes. The existentialist position demands that one confront, and accept, the "anguish" concomitant with assuming responsibility for oneself and all mankind. It demands, according to Sartre, that one cope with the sense of "forlornness" that arises from the recognition that there is no higher authority than man and that there are no permanent values. It demands that one give up the illusion that one's fate is in other hands; in Sartre's terms, it demand that one "despair" of ultimate answers or consequences.

Sartre's essay is, in other words, a position paper. But he does not wish merely to record the tenets of existentialism. His aim is also to convince the reader that existentialism offers a more viable approach to life than other traditional philosophies. Although he seems at times to be trying to justify the hard implications of his philosophy, Sartre is really pointing to the stature that existentialism attains through its bold refusal to deal with anything but intractable reality. He tries, finally, to demonstrate that existentialism encourages one to say, "Think of the possibilities" or "Look what man has made and can make of himself" and thus that existentialism is an optimistic philosophy.

Analytical Considerations

1. Consider how effectively Sartre's various examples illustrate what he means by forlornness, anguish, and despair. For instance, are the discussions of Abraham and the madwoman confusing, or do they clarify the concept of "anguish"?
2. Is the term *despair* ever clearly defined? Does the word describe or mean what Sartre says it does? Would a different word be more appropriate? Explain.
3. What does Sartre mean by his statement that "man is condemned to be free" (paragraph 13)?
4. Discuss the movement of ideas in paragraph 29. Does Sartre contradict himself within the paragraph? Explain how and why.
5. Characterize Sartre's persona in this essay. Does the author come across as a logical and responsible thinker and writer?

Suggested Writing Assignments

1. Compare and contrast Sartre's "Existentialism" with Paul Tillich's "The Riddle of Inequality" (NR 1198, SE 760) as responses to the human situation in the modern world. Do the two share certain values or attitudes? Do they disagree on others?
2. As Sartre delineates it, do you find existentialism a viable approach to life or an appealing philosophy? If so, write an essay discussing its values and the basis of its appeal.
3. Write an essay in response to Sartre's declaration that "Man is nothing else but what he makes of himself."

Additional questions on this essay will be found in the text (NR 1238, SE 769).

Paul Tillich

The Riddle of Inequality

The Norton Reader, p. 1198; Shorter Edition, p. 760

From the viewpoint of Christian belief, the essential inequality of all people is a central paradox, and it is the most painful one of human experience. The paradox or "The Riddle of Inequality," as Paul Tillich calls it, is stated repeatedly in the Gospels: "For to him who has will more be given; and from him who has not, even what he has will be taken away" (Mark iv.25). Like other human mysteries, this riddle cannot be "solved" in the finite world. It must become, rather, a matter of faith to explore the implications of the riddle and to accept, finally and lovingly, the burden of living with(in) the riddle.

Tillich's essay, originally a sermon, takes this Christian approach to the riddle. In a carefully directed analysis, Tillich investigates "the breadth and the depth of the riddle of inequality" (paragraph 1). He divides the investigation into three tightly organized sections. First, he explores what we have and whether or not we really have it; second, he raises the issue of inequality in original gifts (birth, circumstances, etc.); and third, he observes that some people use their talents whereas others do not. These points lead him to the general question "Why has [some thing or other] *not* happened to me?"(paragraph 16). The final four paragraphs of the essay are devoted to positing a way of living with the unsolvable riddle. Tillich finds the "way" not so much in a specific solution, as in his belief in the unity of creation and the participation of the divine in that unity, as symbolically manifested in the cross.

Analytical Considerations

1. What is the "riddle of inequality"? Ask students to formulate it in their own words.
2. What is Tillich's purpose in this essay? Does he have a thesis or is his essay, like Virginia Woolf's "The Death of the Moth" (NR 1214, SE 738), a philosophical and meditative exploration?
3. Does Tillich solve the riddle? On the basis of what certainty? What is the "way" he proposes?
4. Does the essence of Zen Buddhism, as set forth by Gilbert Highet in "The Mystery of Zen" (NR 1205, SE 741), offer a response to the riddle of inequality?

5. What textual clues indicate that this was originally a sermon? How does its origin affect its language and design?
6. Ask students to plot and evaluate the design of "The Riddle." Is Tillich's introduction effective? How has he divided the body of his essay? What techniques serve his purpose? What does Tillich achieve in the last four paragraphs?
7. How does Tillich use rhetorical questions in "The Riddle of Inequality"? Are they overused?
8. Ask students to ponder—and possibly write on—several key statements in this essay:
   A. "The growth of our lives is possible only because we have sacrificed the original gift of innocence.... No maturity is possible without this sacrifice" (paragraph 3).
   B. "In every revolution and in every war, the will to solve the riddle of inequality is a driving force. But neither war nor revolution can remove it" (paragraph 9).
   C. "Each of us must consider the increase or the loss of what is given to him as a matter of his own responsibility" (paragraph 12).
   D. "There is an ultimate unity of all beings, rooted in the divine life from which they come and to which they go. All beings, nonhuman as well as human, participate in it" (paragraph 20).
   E. "In every death which we encounter, something of us dies; in every disease which we encounter, something of us tends to disintegrate" (paragraph 20).
9. How does Tillich weave the imagery as well as the content of the epigraph into his sermon?

Suggested Writing Assignments

1. Write an essay in response to Tillich's assertion "Those talents which are used, even with a risk of losing them, are those which we really have" (paragraph 2).
2. Write an essay in response to any of the key statements in Analytical Consideration 8 or to one of your own choice.
3. Write an essay comparing Tillich's definition of despair—"the inability of getting rid of oneself"—with Jean-Paul Sartre's in "Existentialism" (NR 1229, SE 750). Are their responses to those issues consistently antithetical? Do they have anything in common?